Emergency Services Sector-Specific Plan

An Annex to the National Infrastructure Protection Plan

2010

Homeland Security

Preface

The Emergency Services Sector (ESS) is a system of preparedness, response, and recovery elements that form the Nation's first line of defense for preventing and mitigating the risk from physical and cyber attacks, and manmade and natural disasters. The sector consists of emergency services facilities and associated systems, trained and tested personnel, detailed plans and procedures, redundant systems, and mutual-aid agreements that provide life safety and security services across the Nation via a first-responder community comprised of Federal, State, local, tribal, territorial, and private sector partners. The ESS is a primary "protector" for other critical infrastructure and key resources (CIKR) sectors. The loss or incapacitation of ESS capabilities would notably impact the Nation's security, public safety, and morale.

The Emergency Services Sector-Specific Plan (ES SSP) is an annex to the National Infrastructure Protection Plan (NIPP) and addresses efforts to improve protection of the ESS in an all-hazards environment. The SSP establishes relationships among various government partners at all levels, and between the government and the private sector, to foster the cooperation necessary to improve protection of the sector from natural or manmade disasters.

This 2010 release of the SSP reflects the maturation of the ESS partnership and the progress of the sector programs first outlined in the 2007 SSP. Examples of ESS accomplishments since the publication of the 2007 SSP include:

- Expanded the membership of and participation in the sector partnership;

- Initiated the Emergency Services Sector Information Sharing Working Group and the Information Requirements sub-working group;

- Submitted a R&D capability gap to S&T in collaboration with TSA for Emergency Services and Private Vehicle Operation within a Large, Life-Threatening Toxic Vapor Cloud of Chlorine, leading to a systems study to be conducted in FY 2010;

- Developed a Web-based CIKR Resource Center page for the sector;

- Conducted Webinars on the CIKR Pandemic Influenza Guide; and

- Conducted a Risk Workshop for fixed facilities and have an Emergency Services Self-Assessment Tool (ESSAT) for fixed facilities in development.

On an annual basis, the SSA and sector partners review progress toward verifying, validating, and implementing the goals and objectives as defined in chapter 1 of the SSP. These goals and objectives inform the development and implementation of sector-wide protective programs. Each year, the ESS CIKR Protection Annual Report provides updates on the sector's efforts to identify, prioritize, and coordinate the protection of its critical infrastructure. The SSA, in collaboration with the SCC and GCC, strives to ensure an accurate depiction of the complexities of the sector landscape and that sector goals and priorities are representative of the sector and lead to sector resilience initiatives and protective programs.

The sector's risk mitigation activities (RMAs) are initiatives that involve measures designed to prevent, deter, and mitigate threats; reduce vulnerability to attack or other disasters; minimize consequences; and enable rapid recovery. Examples of key RMAs that carry over to the next fiscal year include:

- **Homeland Security Information Network–Critical Sectors/Emergency Services Sector Portal**

  – Homeland Security Information Network–Critical Sectors/ESS Portal is designed to promote an information-sharing culture that functions in a decentralized, distributed, and coordinated manner, leveraging existing capabilities. The HSIN-CS/ESS Web site began development in FY 2009 with a spring pilot and summer rollout to the entire sector.

- **Emergency Services Self-Assessment Tool**

  – The Enhanced Critical Infrastructure Protection (ECIP) program is designed to assess risks to fixed facilities to compare with risks to like facilities. The Emergency Services Self-Assessment Tool (ESSAT) is being adapted from ECIP in FY 2010, creating an automated risk assessment tool for volunteer use, with an anticipated summer pilot.

Emergency Services Sector Government Coordinating Council Letter of Coordination

The National Infrastructure Protection Plan (NIPP) provides the unifying structure for the integration of critical infrastructure and key resources (CIKR) protection efforts into a single national program. The NIPP provides an overall framework for integrating programs and activities that are underway in the various sectors, as well as new and developing CIKR protection efforts. The NIPP includes 18 Sector-Specific Plans (SSPs) that detail the application of the overall risk management framework to each specific sector.

Each SSP describes a collaborative effort between the private sector; State, local, tribal, and territorial governments; nongovernmental organizations; and the Federal Government. This collaboration will result in the prioritization of protection initiatives and investments within and across sectors to ensure that resources can be applied where they contribute the most to risk mitigation by lowering vulnerabilities, deterring threats, and minimizing the consequences of attacks and other incidents. This document represents the Emergency Services SSP.

By signing this letter, the Emergency Services Government Coordinating Council (GCC) commits to:

- Support SSP concepts and processes, and carry out our assigned functional responsibilities regarding the protection of CIKR as described herein;
- Work with the Secretary of Homeland Security as the Emergency Services Sector-Specific Agency (SSA), as appropriate and consistent with our own agency-specific authorities, resources, and programs, to coordinate funding and implementation of programs that enhance CIKR protection;
- Cooperate and coordinate with the Secretary of Homeland Security as the Emergency Services SSA, in accordance with guidance provided in Homeland Security Presidential Directive 7, as appropriate and consistent with our own agency-specific authorities, resources, and programs, to facilitate CIKR protection;
- Develop or modify existing inter-agency and agency-specific CIKR plans, as appropriate, to facilitate compliance with the Emergency Services SSP;

- Develop and maintain partnerships for CIKR protection with appropriate State, regional, local, tribal, and international entities; private sector owners, operators, associations; and nongovernmental organizations; and

- Protect critical infrastructure information according to the Protected Critical Infrastructure Information Program or other appropriate guidelines, and share CIKR protection-related information, as appropriate and consistent with our own agency-specific authorities and the process described herein.

Signatories

Todd M. Keil

Assistant Secretary
Infrastructure Protection
U.S. Department of Homeland Security

W. Craig Conklin

Director
SSA Executive Management Office
U.S. Department of Homeland Security
Chair, Emergency Services GCC

Emergency Services Sector Coordinating Council Letter of Acknowledgment

The Emergency Services Sector-Specific Plan (SSP), in conjunction with the National Infrastructure Protection Plan (NIPP), provides the unifying Federal structure for the integration of Emergency Services Sector (ESS) critical infrastructure and key resources (CIKR) protection efforts into a single national program. The NIPP provides an overall framework for integrating programs and activities currently underway in the sector, as well as for new and developing CIKR protection efforts. The Emergency Services SSP details how the Federal Government envisions the application to the ESS of the overall risk management framework as outlined in the NIPP.

This SSP describes an effort that will require resources and coordination from Federal, State, local, and tribal governments; the private sector; and nongovernmental organizations in order to achieve the prioritization of protection initiatives and investments across the ESS. This prioritization will support Federal prioritization efforts to ensure that Federal resources are applied where they offer the most benefit for mitigating risk by lowering vulnerabilities, deterring threats, and minimizing the consequences of attacks and other incidents, and encourages a similar risk-based allocation of resources within State and local entities and the private sector.

The complexity of the ESS, along with its unique mission to protect citizens and other sectors creates unique challenges in developing and implementing an SSP. The Sector Coordinating Council (SCC) believes that "protecting the protectors" is critical and is dedicated to working with the community to ensure the protection of its infrastructure, and first and foremost, its personnel. By signing this letter, the members of the Emergency Services SCC do not create an endorsement of the plan, but rather acknowledge that we:

- Will, to the best of our ability, continue to work with the Federal Government, the ESS community, and other sector partners to assist in further development of the SSP in a manner that is supportive of successful and realistic implementation at the responder level;

- Have had some opportunity to provide recommendations and comment on the unique needs, concerns, and perspectives of their organizations or members, which may or may not be reflected in the final document;

- Will, to the best of our ability, maintain partnerships for CIKR protection with appropriate Federal, State, local, tribal, and international entities; other private sector entities; and nongovernmental organizations, so long as such partnerships add value to meeting the needs of responders in the field;

- Will work with the U.S. Department of Homeland Security and the ESS to find suitable and realistic mechanisms to share CIKR protection-related information; and

- Understand that our participation creates no legally binding agreements or liabilities.

Sincerely,

John Thompson

Chair
Emergency Services Sector Coordinating Council

Table of Contents

List of Figures

List of Tables

Executive Summary

The Emergency Services Sector (ESS) is a system of preparedness, response, and recovery elements that forms the Nation's first line of defense for preventing and mitigating the risk from physical and cyber attacks, and manmade and natural disasters. The sector consists of emergency services facilities and associated systems, trained and tested personnel, detailed plans and procedures, redundant systems, and mutual-aid agreements that provide life safety and security services across the Nation via a first-responder community comprised of Federal, State, local, tribal, territorial, and private partners. The ESS is a primary "protector" for other critical infrastructure and key resources (CIKR) sectors. The loss or incapacitation of ESS capabilities would notably impact the Nation's security, public safety, and morale.

The Emergency Services Sector-Specific Plan (SSP) is an annex to the National Infrastructure Protection Plan (NIPP) and addresses efforts to improve protection of the ESS in an all-hazards environment. The SSP establishes relationships among various government partners at all levels, and between the government and the private sector, to foster the cooperation necessary to improve protection of the sector from natural or manmade disasters. The SSP sets a path forward for the sector to collectively identify and prioritize its facilities and systems, assess risk, implement CIKR protective programs, and measure program effectiveness. This document reflects the collaborative efforts among all of the sector partners that are dedicated to protection of CIKR within the ESS.

The ESS provides a wide range of emergency services that contribute to both steady-state and incident management operations with a primary mission to save lives, protect property and the environment, assist communities impacted by disasters and aid recovery from emergency situations. The 2010 SSP reflects the collaborative efforts among sector partners to articulate further the CIKR complexities of the sector. The ESS is further defined by the following five disciplines and six specialized capabilities that make up the sector.

ESS Disciplines	ESS Specialized Capabilities
• *Law Enforcement*	• *Hazardous Materials*
• *Fire and Emergency Services*	• *Search and Rescue*
• *Emergency Management*	• *Explosive Ordnance Disposal*
• *Emergency Medical Services*	• *Special Weapons and Tactics and Tactical Operations*
• *Public Works*	• *Aviation Units*
	• *Public Safety Answering Points*

These functions tend to be organized at the State, local, tribal, and territorial levels of government. Moreover, they form the nucleus of a system of response elements that act as America's first line of defense against terrorist attacks or natural hazards.

Although there are several distinct functions or disciplines that comprise the ESS, many personnel are cross-trained and are qualified to provide service to multiple disciplines in the ESS. This cross-training provides a great deal of flexibility and back-up for the ESS, but careful accounting of personnel is necessary to avoid "double-counting" true capacity in the event that all functions are needed concurrently. Each of these disciplines and capabilities contributes to successful performance of the ESS' vital functions.

Seven distinguishing characteristics help to define the ESS as a CIKR sector. These characteristics contribute to the sector profile and represent important factors for consideration in addressing sector security:

- The most critical feature of the sector is its large, geographically distributed base of facilities, equipment, and highly skilled personnel who provide services in both paid and volunteer capacities;

- It is largely organized at the State, local, tribal, and territorial levels of government, corresponding to the scales on which emergencies generally occur. The complex and dispersed nature of the sector makes it difficult to disable the entire system, but it also presents challenges in coordinating emergency responses across disciplines, regions, and levels of government;

- It relies heavily on complex communication and information technology systems to enable robust communications and appropriate coordination and management of diverse elements during emergency situations;

- It utilizes specialized transportation vehicles and secure transportation routes to facilitate sector operations because personnel, equipment, aid, and victims must be moved to and from scenes of emergencies;

- It has dependencies and interdependencies with multiple CIKR sectors and the National Response Framework's Emergency Support Functions that supply elements for the operation and protection of ESS assets;

- The sector focuses primarily on the protection of other sectors and people, rather than protecting the sector itself, which presents unique challenges in addressing the protection of Emergency Services (ES) as a CIKR sector; and

- ES involves primarily the public sector, but also includes private sector holdings, such as industrial fire departments, sworn private security officers, and private EMS providers.

A variety of entities within the public and private sectors play key roles in securing the ESS. The NIPP sector partnership model facilitates coordination among these entities, with the ES Sector-Specific Agency (SSA) tasked with managing the overall process for building partnerships and leveraging sector security expertise, relationships, and resources through the sector partnership model. The primary Federal partners are represented on the ESS Government Coordinating Council (GCC), which is chaired by the U.S. Department of Homeland Security (DHS) and includes members from DHS, the U.S. Department of Health and Human Services, the U.S. Department of Transportation, the U.S. Department of Justice, and the American Red Cross, among others.

The ES Sector Coordinating Council (SCC) includes the public and private sectors and is comprised of several associations that represent the major functions of the ESS.

SCC Association Members include:

- **National Sheriffs' Association**

- **International Association of Chiefs of Police**

- **International Association of Emergency Managers**

- **International Association of Fire Chiefs**

- **National Association of State EMS Officials**

- **National Emergency Management Association**

- **Security Industry Association**

- **American Ambulance Association**

- **American Public Works Association**

- **Central Station Alarm Association**

- **National Association of Security Companies**

- **National Association of State Fire Marshalls**

- **National Native American Law Enforcement Association**

Emergency Services Sector Goals

1. Partnership Engagement

2. Situational Awareness

3. Prevention, Preparedness, and Protection

4. Sustainability, Resiliency, and Reconstitution

In addition to providing an effective means of information sharing across myriad stakeholder organizations, the ES SCC facilitates the identification and leveraging of existing protective programs and provides a venue for stakeholders to contribute their technical expertise. In addition to the SCC and GCC, the sector also collaborates with other State, regional, and local partners through the State, Local, Tribal, and Territorial Government Coordinating Council, the Regional Consortium Coordinating Council, and Local Emergency Planning Committees to ensure a wide variety of stakeholder perspectives are represented.

Vision Statement for the Emergency Services Sector

An Emergency Services Sector in which facilities, key support systems, information and coordination systems, and personnel are protected from both ordinary operational risks and from extraordinary risks or attacks; ensuring timely, coordinated all-hazards emergency response and public confidence in the sector.

To best support the NIPP and to achieve a secure, protected, and resilient ESS, the SSA collaborates with sector partners to develop goals to inform initiatives reflecting the sector's preparedness and protection needs. Each goal has associated objectives and milestones to enable progress to be measured.

In order to effectively manage protective efforts using a risk-based approach, the ESS first needs to identify the assets, systems, and networks that comprise it. The SSP describes the framework that will be used to accomplish the effort. Sector data comprehensively consider the physical, cyber, and human elements of assets, systems, and networks essential to the ESS.

The SSP also describes a methodology for collecting, verifying, and updating ESS facilities and systems data to ensure completeness and accuracy. Information on ESS CIKR is maintained by DHS in the Infrastructure Data Warehouse (IDW). DHS will continue working with sector partners to refine the taxonomy used to categorize the assets associated with the ESS in the IDW. DHS and the SSAs will also continue to work with Federal, State, local, and tribal governments, as well as the private sector, to ensure that the inventory data structure is accurate, complete, and secure.

The cornerstone of both the NIPP and the SSP is the risk management framework, which establishes the processes for evaluating consequence, vulnerability, and threat information to produce a comprehensive, systematic, and rational assessment of national, sector, and individual asset, system, network, or function risk. Three general risk assessment layers, listed in increasing complexity, are utilized when examining risk for the sector: (1) facility-specific or fixed assets, (2) specialized emergency services assets or systems, and (3) multiple systems in a region or multiple regions. This layered approach for assessing risk utilizes an existing vulnerability assessment framework and builds on it by enhancing and customizing the vulnerability component and adding sector-specific threat and consequence components.

A variety of assessment methodologies are used by partners throughout the ESS. Currently, the Office of Infrastructure Protection's Protective Security Advisors conduct Enhanced Critical Infrastructure Protection (ECIP) assessments at select ESS locations. The ECIP assessment is designed to assess overall site security, identify gaps, recommend protective measures, educate facility owners and operators on security, and promote communication and information sharing among facility owners and operators, DHS, and State governments. In addition, a Risk Assessment Working Group was established at the request of State and local stakeholders to further examine the ECIP and discuss risk assessment associated with critical elements in the ESS and its subcomponents.

The final assessment component, which measures consequences, is not yet developed, but will be based on identifying consequences that are adjustable and appropriate for the relevant asset. A Web-based Emergency Services Self Assessment Tool (ESSAT) is envisioned to be the product that can be used by emergency managers, specialty unit leaders, and regional response and planning personnel. When completed, the ESSAT will enable the sector to select and define a region's area of response parameters, threat profile, and consequence profile to assess risk on one or more facility-specific assets (fixed), specialized emergency services assets (systems), or multiple systems in a region or multiple regions.

With the support of sector partners, the ESS will continue to assess the consequences, vulnerabilities, and threats that make up the sector risk profile. This information will be reviewed and updated regularly to reflect the changing environment and its impact on risk.

Due to limited resources, the sector cannot protect every element of its infrastructure against all possible threats. Affordability, return on investment, and sustainability are key considerations in determining which shortfalls require attention. Systematic methods for prioritizing sector assets, as well as any corresponding protective actions, offer direction and increase the defensibility of resource allocation decisions. DHS stresses all-hazards preparedness, which requires attention to a wide range of events and regional geographic and demographic perspectives to risk gaps that drive sector resource requirements in their mitigation. Each factor (threat, vulnerability, or consequence) of the risk equation and the relative importance of existing risk gaps are also considered when determining prioritization of protective initiatives. Facility asset risk mitigation will most generally be prioritized by the respective facility manager, emergency service leader, or emergency manager, while system asset risk mitigation prioritization is expected to be done by the individual system director or manager, or regional emergency manager/planner. As the risk environment changes, asset prioritization will be reviewed and updated accordingly.

The ES SSA coordinates with sector partners to facilitate the effective implementation of numerous protective programs that manage risk by focusing on the four aspects of the NIPP Protective Spectrum: deter, detect, devalue, and defend. This approach ensures that risk is managed effectively by deterring threats, mitigating vulnerabilities, and minimizing consequences of all-hazards incidents. The ESS concentrates on protective programs that support the resilience of the sector by encompassing several areas such as skill proficiency, information sharing, cooperative agreements, and infrastructure resilience.

As a nonregulated sector, the majority of these programs are voluntary and dependent on the funding and resources of participating stakeholders. The broad diversity within the sector and the desire of owners and operators to strengthen their protective programs are reflected in the breadth of initiatives undertaken by sector partners. They include an array of activities such as developing mutual-aid agreements to share resources, promoting information sharing and developing training programs, initiating active or passive countermeasures, installing security systems, promoting workforce security programs, and implementing cybersecurity measures, among others. In addition, Federal, State, local, and tribal governments have sponsored a broad range of complementary protective programs including vulnerability and risk assessment processes and methodologies.

Key Protective Program Areas

- *Information-sharing initiatives*
- *Training and certification courses*
- *Mutual Aid Agreements*
- *Cybersecurity working groups and cross-sector collaboration*

The ES SSA is developing a comprehensive listing of the CIKR protection initiatives, activities, and training programs that impact the first responder community.

This will be accomplished through the active participation of practitioners and sector partners in the collection of protective programs utilizing the Sector Initiatives Questionnaire, the outcome of which will be shared with all sector partners across each discipline and specialized capability.

The NIPP uses a metrics-based performance evaluation system to measure progress and provide a basis for establishing account-ability, documenting actual performance, facilitating diagnoses, and promoting effective management. The metrics supply the data to confirm that specific goals are being met and to show which corrective actions may be required to continue to meet those goals.

The ESS meets NIPP metrics program requirements by identifying protective programs that are key risk mitigation activities and developing metrics to measure their progress. These metrics are divided into descriptive data, output data, and outcome data to account for the various aspects of each activity's progress. The ES SSA works collaboratively with sector partners to collect and verify metrics data, and compare the sector's performance with its goals. The SSA and its sector partners can adjust and adapt the sector CIKR protection approach to account for progress achieved, identify areas of improvement, and recognize opportunities to further develop the sector goals and objectives. This approach promotes continuous improvement by using the data garnered from collection and measurement efforts to inform protective program implementation and development.

Research and development (R&D) plays a significant role in enabling homeland security partners to develop knowledge and technologies that more effectively reduce risk to the Nation's CIKR. ESS is made up of very diverse disciplines and supporting elements with missions that address a wide variety of terrorist and natural threats to the homeland. New and innovative technology-based solutions are required to prevent or mitigate the potential effects of current and future dangers, including the numerous challenges faced by the disciplines and supporting elements that are integral to providing protection for the sector. Generally, the CIKR R&D focus for the sector is to influence R&D activities at the Federal level, furthering a comprehensive approach that encompasses both operational and CIKR R&D needs. Continuous focus on R&D efforts is needed to improve protection of the Nation's emergency responders and supporting facilities and systems in an all-hazards environment. Advances in technology enable emergency responders, as well as the entities supporting them, to adequately prepare for, quickly respond to, and effectively recover from terrorist attacks, natural disasters, and other catastrophic incidents.

Using a requirements-driven, output-oriented methodology, R&D entities, such as DHS' Science and Technology Directorate and the Interagency Board's Science Technology Committee, identify responder requirements and develop and integrate technologies aligned with the priorities of the first responder community.

The ES SSA is the sector lead for coordinating protective programs and resilience strategies in partnership with CIKR stakeholders. It is tasked with maintaining and updating the SSP, spearheading the annual reporting process, and coordinating sector training, education, and information-sharing mechanisms.

DHS, in collaboration with CIKR partners, will foster sector partnerships to coordinate infrastructure protection on various levels through the GCC, SCC, and various working groups. DHS will also promote information sharing through a variety of channels, including the Homeland Security Information Network and other established sector information-sharing networks.

The SSP provides a coordinated, sector-specific approach that remains attentive, balanced, and flexible as new developments emerge. The sector will have the opportunity to review and revise the SSP annually, as needed, to reflect changes in the sector's protective posture or processes. The SSP will be rewritten every three years in conjunction with the NIPP review and revision process. This implementation of the sector partnership model bolsters sector protection and resilience by maintaining a forum for information sharing and collaboration, program implementation and development, and transparency.

Introduction

Protecting and ensuring continuity of U.S. critical infrastructure and key resources (CIKR) is essential to the Nation's security, public health and safety, economic vitality, and way of life. CIKR includes the assets, systems, and networks that provide vital services to the Nation. Terrorist attacks and other manmade or natural disasters could significantly disrupt the functioning of government and business alike, and produce cascading effects far beyond the affected CIKR and physical location of the incident. Direct and indirect impacts could include large-scale human casualties, property destruction, economic disruption, and significant degradation of national morale and public confidence. Terrorist attacks using components of the Nation's CIKR as weapons of mass destruction (WMD) could have even more devastating physical, psychological, and economic consequences.

Protection for the sector includes actions to mitigate the overall risk to physical, cyber, and human CIKR assets, systems, networks, or their interconnecting links that may potentially result from exposure, injury, destruction, incapacitation, or exploitation. In the context of the National Infrastructure Protection Plan (NIPP), this includes actions to deter threats, mitigate vulnerabilities, or minimize consequences associated with all-hazards incidents. Protection can include a wide range of activities, such as improving operating protocols, hardening facilities, building resilience and redundancy, initiating active or passive countermeasures, leveraging self-healing technologies, promoting workforce surety programs, and implementing cybersecurity measures. The NIPP and its complementary Sector-Specific Plans (SSPs) provide a consistent, unifying structure for integrating both existing and future CIKR protection efforts. The NIPP also provides the core processes and mechanisms that enable all levels of government and private sector partners to work together to implement CIKR protection effectively and efficiently.

The NIPP was developed through extensive coordination with partners at all levels of government and the private sector. NIPP processes are designed to be adapted and tailored to individual sector and partner requirements. Implementation of the NIPP enables the government and private sector to use collective expertise and experience to more clearly define CIKR protection issues and practical solutions, and to ensure that existing CIKR protection approaches and efforts, including business continuity and resilience planning, are recognized.

Purpose

The NIPP requires each CIKR sector to develop an SSP to provide a framework for reducing risk and fostering cooperation and information sharing among sector partners, including all levels of government, the private sector, and international partners. The Emergency Services SSP follows and supports the risk management approach and key steps outlined in the NIPP:

- Setting sector goals;
- Identifying the sector's CIKR assets, systems, and networks;
- Identifying and assessing potential risks based on threats, vulnerabilities, and consequences;
- Prioritizing assets based on risk, and prioritizing protection initiatives on a cost-benefit basis;

- Developing and implementing sustainable programs to protect assets;

- Using metrics to measure and communicate the effectiveness of SSP implementation; and

- Fostering and informing sector research and development initiatives, and communicating partner requirements.

The SSP will be reviewed periodically to ensure that preparedness efforts remain effective, efficient, and correspond to sector risk. This review process will include input from various sector officials, including representatives from the private sector and multiple government agencies. In addition to regular reviews, the SSP will be reissued every three years. Changes may also be made to the document on an as-needed basis to address changes in the risk environment or lessons learned from actual events and exercises.

Figure I-1 shows the interaction of core elements of the NIPP based on a dynamic risk environment, with threat information provided by the U.S. Department of Homeland Security (DHS). The resulting outputs are sector-specific strategies for protecting assets based on sector priorities. The ultimate objective of the SSP is to have Federal, State, local, tribal and territorial governments and the private sector work with the Sector-Specific Agency (SSA) to implement the plan in a way that is consistent, sustainable, effective, and measurable.

Figure I-1: NIPP Risk Management Framework

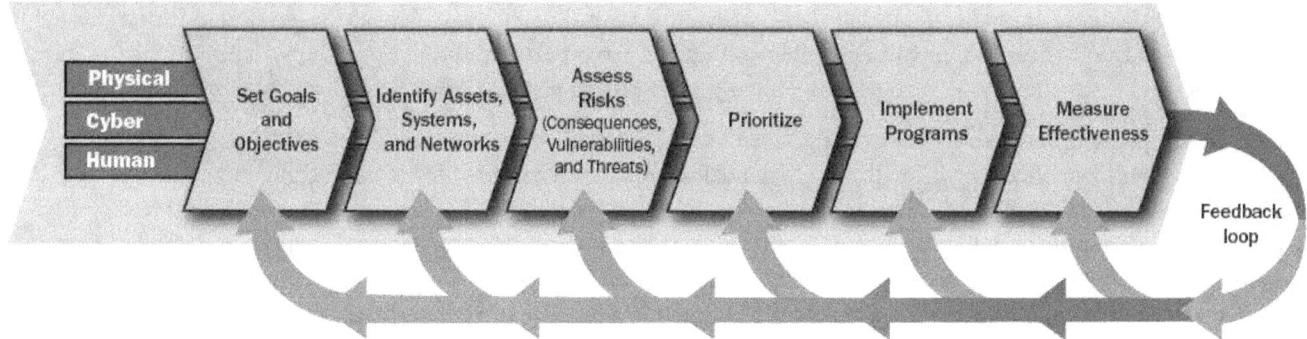

Continuous Improvement to enhance protection of CIKR

The SSP provides a detailed description of the specific processes used to identify, assess, prioritize, and protect CIKR; processes used to measure effectiveness; the approach required to implement protective activities, including descriptions of projects, initiatives, activities, timeframes, milestones, and resources. The purpose of this document is to describe the efforts through which Emergency Services Sector (ESS) assets, systems, and networks are protected. Continued implementation of the programs and processes described in the SSP enable Federal, State, local, tribal, and territorial governments and the private sector to work together to protect the sector. Nothing in this SSP is intended to alter or impede the ability of any of these partners to perform their respective responsibilities under the law.

Changes from 2007 Sector-Specific Plan

The SSP is a living document, updated regularly to reflect changes in the NIPP, sector composition and structure, as well as the evolving priorities of sector stakeholders. This section discusses the most notable changes since the 2007 SSP.

Resilience, All Hazards, and Cybersecurity

The 2010 SSP builds on previous plans, but reflects the 2009 NIPP's increased emphasis on resilience, all hazards, and cybersecurity. By focusing on security and preparedness from the all-hazards approach, the sector can use prevention, protection, and response capabilities not only to reduce the threat of a terrorist attack on its assets, but also to prevent or mitigate damage in the event of a natural or unintentional manmade disaster. This comprehensive approach strengthens the sector so that it is fully prepared to face the challenges ahead. The SSA, working in conjunction with DHS, other Federal agencies, and additional sector partners, ensures seamless linkage between the NIPP and steady-state protection and incident management activities.

Sector Goals and Objectives

The revised goals and objectives included in this document more clearly reflect the priorities of the sector and represent the sector's view of how best to support the overarching goal of the NIPP to achieve a secure, protected, and resilient Emergency Services Sector (ESS). These goals underline the sector's emphasis on protecting the human assets as well as the physical and cyber assets of the sector. Alignment of the sector's priorities with the documented goals and objectives ensures consistent priorities and a common operating picture, which in turn enhances a coordinated approach to infrastructure protection within the ESS.

Sector Disciplines

Since 2007, the ES SSA has reevaluated the sector's discipline categories. The ESS has defined itself along five broad disciplines: 1) Law Enforcement, 2) Fire and Emergency Services, 3) Emergency Medical Services, 4) Emergency Management, and 5) Public Works. Supplementing these disciplines and overall sector operations are specialized capabilities specific to the ESS: Hazardous Materials (HAZMAT), Search and Rescue (SAR), Explosive Ordnance Disposal (EOD), Special Weapons and Tactics and Tactical Operations (SWAT), Aviation Units, and Public Safety Answering Points (PSAPs). The physical, cyber, and human critical infrastructure that support and comprise each ESS discipline and specialized capabilities define the parameters for information collection and infrastructure identification. These updated disciplines and capabilities enhance the sector's ability to define its assets, collect information, and further develop sector taxonomy, as well as ensure that the various components are best represented in meetings and initiatives falling under the Critical Infrastructure Partnership Advisory Council (CIPAC) framework.

Risk Assessment

To facilitate accurate and efficient risk assessment and analysis, sector representatives have identified three general risk assessment layers: (1) facility-specific or fixed assets, (2) specialized emergency services assets or systems, and (3) multiple systems in a region or multiple regions. As with risk assessment in general, each risk assessment layer has individual aspects of prioritization, yet builds on the other layers, rolling up multiple systems into a regional perspective. Facility risk priorities generally relate to an individual facility (e.g., fire or police stations, 9-1-1 call centers, or emergency operations centers). System risk priorities generally relate to the elements that build the system and the entities that rely on and manage the 9-1-1 call centers, HAZMAT, or SWAT teams. Regional risk priorities relate to multiple systems and multiple echelons of concern. This updated approach provides valuable information to inform the development of protective programs and the allocation of resources.

1. Sector Profile, Sector Partners, and Goals

The ESS provides a wide range of emergency services that contribute to both steady-state and incident management operations. The 2010 SSP reflects the collaborative efforts among sector partners to articulate further the CIKR complexities of the sector while also clearly identifying the critical elements that make up the sector profile. This chapter describes the revised sector profile, beginning with the ES mission and a description of the different emergency services disciplines. The chapter then examines these disciplines with respect to several key components of each, including equipment and facilities (physical), information technology and communications systems (cyber), and people (human). Additionally, the chapter defines the specialized capabilities that exist across disciplines and incorporates them into the sector's profile. The attributes relative to the disciplines and the specialized capabilities are combined to form the basis for the assets, systems, and networks that further define the sector.

The revised goals and objectives included in this chapter more clearly reflect the priorities of the sector and represent the sector's view of how best to support the overarching goal of the NIPP to achieve a secure, protected, and resilient ESS. These goals underline the sector's emphasis on protecting the human as well as physical assets of the sector. Finally, the chapter identifies sector partners, their roles and responsibilities, and describes the sector's goals and desired long-term protective posture.

Figure 1-1: National Infrastructure Protection Plan (NIPP) Risk Management Framework: Set Sector Goals

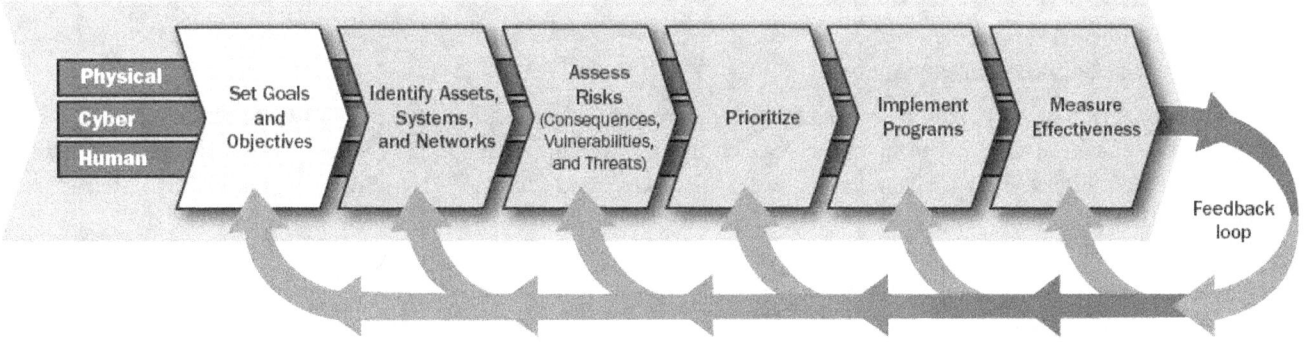

Continuous Improvement to enhance protection of CIKR

1.1 Sector Profile

The primary mission of the ESS is to save lives, protect property and the environment, assist communities impacted by disasters and aid recovery during emergencies. The ESS is comprised of assets, systems, and networks that encompass the physical, cyber, and human components of CIKR.

ESS is defined by the five disciplines that make up the sector: 1) Law Enforcement, 2) Fire and Emergency Services, 3) Emergency Management, 4) Emergency Medical Services, and 5) Public Works. In addition to these disciplines, there are specialized capabilities: Hazardous Materials (HAZMAT), Search and Rescue (SAR), Explosive Ordnance Disposal (EOD), Special Weapons and Tactics and Tactical Operations (SWAT), Aviation Units, and Public Safety Answering Points (PSAPs). Each of these disciplines and capabilities contributes to successful performance of the vital functions of the ESS. These functions tend to be organized at the State, local, tribal, and territorial levels of government. Moreover, they form the nucleus of a system of response elements that act as America's first line of defense against terrorist attacks or natural hazards.

Seven distinguishing characteristics help to define the ESS as a CIKR sector. These characteristics contribute to the sector profile and represent important factors for consideration in addressing sector security:

- The most critical feature of the sector is its large, geographically distributed base of facilities, equipment, and highly skilled personnel who provide services in both paid and volunteer capacities;

- The sector is organized primarily at the State, local, tribal, and territorial levels of government, corresponding to the scales on which emergencies generally occur. The complex and dispersed nature of the sector makes it difficult to disable the entire system, but it also presents challenges in coordinating emergency responses across disciplines, regions, and levels of government;

- The sector relies heavily on complex communication and information technology (IT) systems to enable robust communications and appropriate coordination and management of diverse elements during emergencies;

- The sector relies on secure transportation routes which are critical for use by first responders with specialized vehicles to provide aid and move equipment and personnel to and from scenes of emergency;

- The sector has dependencies and interdependencies with multiple CIKR sectors and the National Response Framework's Emergency Support Functions that supply elements for both operations and protection of ESS assets;

- The sector focuses primarily on protecting other sectors and people, rather than protecting the sector itself, which presents unique challenges in addressing the protection of ES as a CIKR; and

- ESS involves primarily the public sector, but also includes private sector holdings, such as industrial fire departments, sworn private security officers, and private EMS providers.

1.1.1 Emergency Services Components

The ESS consists of physical, cyber, and human elements that make up the assets, systems, and networks of the sector. Physical elements include facilities and equipment; cyber elements include cyber infrastructure related to information management systems and technology; and human elements include trained career and volunteer personnel. The elements are described in detail below.

Physical Element

The physical elements of each of the ESS disciplines consist of a wide variety of assets integral to the daily operational requirements of the sector. Each discipline within the ESS has a unique list of physical elements that contribute to its services. Across the sector, the elements typically consist of facilities used in daily operations, support, training, or storage, as well as equipment and vehicles critical to the discipline. Each discipline requires a wide variety of specialized equipment and vehicles in order for the sector to perform its mission. To ensure safe and effective operation of this equipment, extensive training of personnel is often necessary. Additionally, emergency communications critical to daily operations, such as land mobile radio systems, are a substantial physical component in any agency.

Cyber Element

Cybersecurity, as defined by the 2009 NIPP, includes prevention of damage to, unauthorized use of, or exploitation of electronic information and communications systems and the information contained therein to ensure confidentiality, integrity, and availability. Given the increasing interconnected nature and inherent complexity of IT and cyber systems, cyber-related issues are a major concern for the sector and are reflected in the sector's goals and objectives. Many ESS activities, such as emergency operations communications, database management, biometric activities, telecommunications, and electronic systems (e.g., security systems), are conducted by partners virtually. These activities are vulnerable to cyber attack. Additionally, the Internet is widely used by the sector to provide information as well as alerts, warnings, and threats relevant to the ESS. Systems include those established by the DHS, such as the Homeland Security Information Network (HSIN), the Federal Emergency Management Agency's (FEMA) National Response Coordination Center (NRCC), the National Infrastructure Coordinating Center (NICC), the National Operations Center (NOC), the Emergency Management and Response Information Sharing and Analysis Center (EMR-ISAC), and the Homeland Infrastructure Threat and Risk Analysis Center (HITRAC). Additionally, virtual systems include those established by other Federal agencies, including the National Oceanic and Atmospheric Administration (NOAA) and the National Weather Service (NWS); and State, local, and regional agencies. For example, WEB-EOC is used by some State Offices of Emergency Management. Additionally, agencies may rely on commercial Web-based situation-status and resource management platforms. Computer-aided Dispatch (CAD) systems, such as 9-1-1 Dispatch Systems, risk degradation of response capability if connectivity to the Internet is lost.

ESS requires interoperable networks that are reliable as well as redundant. These cyber-related elements are so essential to emergency responders that security in any individual facility must be considered in the risk analysis process. Degradation of these systems would significantly raise the overall risk to a facility and the emergency responder, and could impact the ability of the sector to carry out its mission effectively.

The nature of the ESS makes broad generalization of cyber system usage difficult. Although some similarities exist, each discipline (defined in section 1.1.2) uses cyber systems differently in its daily activities. A lack of standards, combined with variations in organization, diversity of assets, availability of resources, and other factors, creates a very diverse and dynamic cyber landscape. Therefore, the sector has established an ESS Cyber Security Working Group (CSWG) whose focus is to recommend and implement protective measures and provide tools and resources for the agency to conduct inventory assessments and audits of cyber assets and networks.

A variety of mechanisms, including the Multi-State Information Sharing and Analysis Center (MS-ISAC), the United States Computer Emergency Readiness Team (US-CERT), and the Cross-Sector Cyber Security Working Group (CSCSWG), help to inform the ESS about cyber-related risks to the sector. Established in January 2003, the MS-ISAC is a voluntary, collaborative effort by State and local governments to facilitate communication regarding cyber and critical infrastructure readiness and response efforts. The State of New York's Office of Cybersecurity and Critical Infrastructure Coordination coordinates the MS-ISAC, which DHS has recognized for its proactive role in bringing the States together. The MS-ISAC provides the ESS with a common mechanism for raising the level of cybersecurity readiness and response within the sector. It also provides a central resource for gathering information from the sector regarding cyber threats to critical infrastructure. The MS-ISAC publishes and electronically disseminates daily cyber-related bulletins to ESS constituents. The EMR-ISAC also delivers bulletins to more than 40,000 sector participants and disseminates information nationally through State and local fusion centers.

Although each individual CIKR sector addresses its own sector-specific, cyber-related issues, an integrated cross-sector cybersecurity perspective is also needed to address the mutual concerns and issues that span numerous sectors. This cross-sector perspective facilitates the sharing of information and knowledge about various cybersecurity concerns, such as common vulnerabilities and protective measures, and leverages functional cyber expertise in a comprehensive forum. To meet this need, the DHS Assistant Secretary for Cybersecurity and Communications proposed, and the Partnership for Critical Infrastructure Security (PCIS) agreed, to establish the CSCSWG under the auspices of the CIPAC. The CSCSWG is a public-private collaboration that serves as a forum to bring government and the private sector together to address cyber-related risk across the CIKR sectors. The ES SSA is an active participant in the CSCSWG's monthly meetings.

Human Element

The sector's most important CIKR is the safety of the emergency responder or human asset, the protection of which is almost indistinguishable from the emergency responder's mission to protect the public. Protection of the human asset within ESS is multifaceted and includes highly specialized skill sets or capabilities that require extensive training and specialized equipment.

The ESS consists of hundreds of thousands of career and volunteer men and women in all disciplines who serve in every community in the United States. These individuals contribute to the safety and security of the Nation by saving lives, preparing for and managing response operations, protecting residents and property, and ensuring community order in times of disaster.

1.1.2 Emergency Services Disciplines

The ESS encompasses a wide range of emergency response functions through a variety of roles. The NIPP defines critical infrastructure preparedness functions as "the service, process, capability, or operation performed by specific infrastructure assets, systems, or networks." In the ESS, the following five distinct disciplines coincide with this definition of functions:

1. Law Enforcement
2. Fire and Emergency Services
3. Emergency Medical Services
4. Emergency Management
5. Public Works

Although there are five distinct disciplines that comprise the ESS, many personnel may be qualified in one or more specialized capabilities that exist within or between disciplines. For example, HAZMAT team members are typically members of fire service or law enforcement who are also trained to perform advanced HAZMAT capabilities. This provides a great deal of flexibility for the ESS, but careful accounting of personnel is necessary to avoid double-counting the sector's true capacity in the event that all disciplines are needed concurrently.

Finally, it is important to note that, for the purposes of the ESS, representatives from each of these disciplines come together to develop security plans and protective measures that will benefit the sector as a whole. Although the individual disciplines each have their own duties and priorities, these disciplines come together through the partnership framework of the NIPP to speak with one voice and collaborate on critical security and preparedness issues.

Table 1-1: Roles and Responsibilities for ESS Functions and Disciplines

Function/Discipline	Roles and Responsibilities
Law Enforcement	Maintaining law and order and protecting the public from harm. Law enforcement activities may include investigation, prevention, response, court security, and detention, as well as other associated capabilities and duties.
Fire and Emergency Services	Prevention and minimizing loss of life and property during incidents resulting from fire, medical emergencies, and other all-hazards events.
Emergency Medical Services	Providing emergency medical assessment and treatment at the scene of an incident, during an infectious disease outbreak, or during transport and delivery of injured or ill personnel to a treatment facility as part of an organized EMS system.
Emergency Management	Leading efforts to mitigate, prepare for, respond to, and recover from all types of multijurisdictional incidents.
Public Works	Providing essential emergency functions, such as assessing damage to buildings, roads and bridges; clearing, removing and disposing of debris; restoring utility services; and managing emergency traffic.

Law Enforcement

The law enforcement discipline of the ESS includes law enforcement personnel and law enforcement agencies (LEAs), and the physical and cyber assets, systems, and networks that support it. Law enforcement facilities contain the personnel, equipment, and vehicles used to protect the public, enforce the law, conduct criminal investigations, gather evidence, and apprehend perpetrators of crimes.

LEAs are Federal, State, local, tribal, and territorial-level government organizations charged with serving their communities and contributing to the public safety and quality of life by maintaining law and order and protecting the general public from harm. This encompasses a broad range of activities associated with the authority to enforce Federal and State criminal laws. Law enforcement officers are responsible for preventing and investigating criminal acts and apprehending and detaining individuals suspected or convicted of criminal offenses. Law enforcement personnel include not only police officers, sheriffs, State troopers, State patrols, and State police, but also criminal investigators, SWAT and tactical units, bomb squads, HAZMAT personnel, and Federal enforcement agents and officers.

Fire and Emergency Services

The Fire and Emergency Services discipline involves highly trained personnel tasked with minimizing loss of life and property during incidents that result from fire, medical emergencies, HAZMAT releases, terrorist attacks, natural disasters, and other emergencies. Fire and Emergency Services personnel are trained in firefighting and rescue techniques; however, many fire and emergency services personnel also have additional training in wildland firefighting, emergency medical services, various types of search and rescue, hazardous materials response, and/or explosive ordnance disposal.

Although career firefighters protect a large portion of the population, roughly three-quarters of the firefighters in the United States are volunteers. Firefighters support emergency response efforts at the Federal, State, local, tribal, and territorial levels of government and can function as a part of mutual-aid elements for surrounding jurisdictions. The fire service has a robust and rapidly growing mutual aid network, which includes both physical and human elements. This function is traditionally carried out by public sector employees, but there are a number of private sector departments (e.g., industrial) or contractors (e.g., wildland fire responders) across the country.

Emergency Medical Services

Emergency Medical Services (EMS) systems consist of emergency medical care provided at the scene of an incident, during an infectious disease outbreak, and during patient transport and delivery to a hospital or other treatment facilities. Responses to incidents include handling the triage, treatment, and transport of all injured and ill patients; taking appropriate steps to protect staff, patients, facilities, and the environment; and helping to monitor response teams while providing needed comprehensive medical care and mental health support to patients and their families.

EMS system capabilities within the sector include appropriately dispatching EMS resources; providing feasible, suitable, and medically acceptable pre-hospital triage and treatment of patients; and providing transport and medical care en route to the appropriate receiving treatment facility as well as initial patient tracking. EMS systems include highly skilled emergency medical technicians and paramedics as well as highly sophisticated emergency medical vehicles, such as air and ground ambulances, that provide equipment, supplies, and transport for injured patients. Many EMS personnel are cross-trained as firefighters, and similar to fire and emergency services, include both career and volunteer personnel.

Emergency Management

Emergency management programs are responsible for providing overall pre-disaster planning and other programs, such as training and exercises for natural and manmade disasters that can affect a community. These programs are the first line of defense in coordinating a large-scale event in any community to ensure effective response and recovery. Utilizing an all-hazards approach, the emergency management function in the ESS is carried out by a combination of partners that represent Federal, State, local, tribal, and territorial levels of government; nongovernmental organizations (NGOs); and private organizations and agencies.

Emergency Operations Center (EOC) management is the capability to provide multiagency coordination for incident management by activating and operating an EOC for a pre-planned or no-notice event. EOC management includes EOC activation, notification, staffing, and deactivation; management, direction, control, and coordination of response and recovery activities; coordination of efforts among neighboring governments at each level and among local, regional, State, and Federal EOCs; coordination of public information and warning; and maintenance of the information and communication necessary for coordinating response and recovery activities. Similar entities may include the National (or Regional) Response Coordination Center (NRCC or RRCC), Joint Field Offices (JFO), NOC, Joint Operations Center (JOC), Multi-Agency Coordination Center (MACC), and the Initial Operating Facility (IOF).

Public Works

Public works provides essential emergency response services, such as assessing damage to buildings, roads and bridges; clearing, removing, and disposing of debris; restoring utility services; and managing emergency traffic. With responsibility for hardening security enhancements to critical facilities and monitoring the safety of public water supplies, public works is an integral component of a jurisdiction's emergency planning efforts. Additionally, public works departments supply heavy machinery, raw materials, and emergency operators, all of which are critical to daily community maintenance and preparedness. To supplement its own resources or to bolster those of another agency in an emergency, public works often enters into mutual aid agreements with other communities or States to provide personnel, equipment and materials during a response effort. Public works may also manage contracts for additional labor, equipment, or services that may be needed during an event.

1.1.3 Emergency Services Specialized Capabilities

The capabilities outlined below represent critical activities that contribute to overall operations of the ESS. Some of these capabilities are found within specific disciplines of the sector; others may be found in several disciplines. These specialized capabilities are often part of mutual-aid agreements (MAAs) or emergency management compacts among States or jurisdictions.

Table 1-2: Roles and Responsibilities for ESS Specialized Capabilities

Specialized Capabilities	Roles and Responsibilities
Hazardous Materials Response	Recognizing and responding to Chemical, Biological, Radiologic, Nuclear (CBRN) incidents; establishing mass decontamination sites; and protecting the public, the environment, and property during incidents involving real or potential release of hazardous materials.
Search and Rescue	Providing search and rescue capabilities can vary significantly across jurisdictions, from local heavy and technical rescue units employed for local incidents, to State teams, to the national level response system. A well-organized structure helps ensure coordination and cooperation and that local and national needs are addressed rapidly.
Explosive Ordnance Disposal	Conducting searches to locate hidden bombs, investigating suspicious packages, and if necessary, rendering safe any bombs and ensuring safe disposal.
Special Weapons and Tactics and Tactical Operations	Responding to highly dangerous and critical incidents, and engaging in high-risk services.
Aviation Units	Providing rapid egress into areas not accessible or easily accessible to ground-based assets through the utilization of highly sophisticated equipment. Aviation units also support the ability to identify the scope of an incident, monitor the progression of an incident, or secure against a potential incident, which covers great distance.
Public Safety Answering Points	Providing public and emergency response communications as well as a universal emergency telephone number system (9-1-1) to protect human life, preserve property, and maintain general community security.

Hazardous Materials Capabilities

HAZMAT is the capability to assess and manage the consequences of a hazardous materials release, either accidental or criminal. Critical HAZMAT activities include the following:

- Identifying and testing all likely hazardous substances onsite;

- Ensuring responders have protective clothing and equipment;

- Conducting rescue operations to remove affected victims from the hazardous environment, conducting geographical survey searches of suspected sources or contamination spreads, and establishing isolation perimeters;

- Mitigating the effects of hazardous materials and decontaminating on-site victims, responders, and equipment;

- Coordinating off-site decontamination with relevant agencies; and

- Notifying appropriate environmental, health, and law enforcement agencies to begin implementation of their standard evidence collection and investigation procedures.

To coordinate HAZMAT-related CIKR issues effectively, the ESS must involve other agencies including the U.S. Fire Administration (USFA) and the U.S. Department of Transportation's Pipeline Hazardous Materials Safety Administration (PHMSA). Agencies that affect HAZMAT training and safety requirements include regulatory agencies, such as the Occupational Safety and Health Administration (OSHA); research and investigation agencies, such as the National Institute of Occupational Safety and Health (NIOSH); and standards-setting organizations, such as the National Fire Protection Association (NFPA).

The capability to respond to a HAZMAT incident resides in multiple ESS disciplines, including Fire and Emergency Services, Emergency Medical Services, and Law Enforcement, as well as in the private industries that manufacture or transport hazardous materials.

Search and Rescue

Search and rescue (SAR) capabilities can vary significantly across local, regional, and national jurisdictions. A well-organized structure helps ensure that the ESS addresses local and national needs in a rapid manner. State, tribal, and territorial authorities are responsible for SAR within their respective jurisdictions and should designate a SAR Coordinator to provide integration and coordination of all SAR services. During incidents or potential incidents requiring a unified response, Federal SAR responsibilities reside within primary agencies that provide timely and specialized SAR capabilities. Support agencies provide specific capabilities or resources that support Emergency Support Function 9 (ESF-9).

SAR services include distress monitoring, incident communications, locating distressed personnel, coordination, and execution of rescue operations including extrication or evacuation. It also includes providing medical assistance and civilian services through the use of public and private resources to assist persons and property in potential or actual distress.

Federal SAR response operational environments are classified as:

- **Structural Collapse Urban Search and Rescue**

  Structural collapse SAR includes operation for natural and manmade disasters and catastrophic incidents as well as other structural collapse operations that primarily require FEMA's Urban Search and Rescue (US&R) Response task force operations. The National US&R Response System integrates DHS/FEMA US&R task forces, Incident Support Teams (ISTs), and technical specialists. The Federal Structural Collapse SAR response integrates FEMA task forces in support of unified SAR operations conducted in accordance with the U.S. National Search and Rescue Plan (NSP).

- **Maritime/Coastal/Waterborne Search and Rescue**

  Maritime/Coastal/Waterborne SAR includes operations for natural and manmade disasters that primarily require the U.S. Coast Guard (USCG) air, ship, boat, and response team operations. The Federal Maritime/Coastal/Waterborne SAR response integrates the USCG resources in support of unified SAR operations conducted in accordance with the NSP. Personnel are trained and experienced in Maritime/Coastal/Waterborne SAR operations and possess specialized expertise, facilities, and equipment for conducting an effective response to distress situations. USCG develops, maintains, and operates rescue facilities for SAR in waters subject to U.S. jurisdiction.

- **Inland/Wilderness Search and Rescue**

  Land SAR includes operations that require aviation and ground forces to meet mission objectives other than Maritime/Coastal/Waterborne and structural collapse SAR operations as described above. Land SAR primary agencies will integrate their efforts to provide an array of diverse capabilities under ESF-9. The primary lead agency for Inland/Wilderness SAR is the U.S. Department of the Interior/National Park Service (DOI/NPS). DOI/NPS has SAR resources that are specially trained to operate in various roles including ground search, small boat operations, swift water rescue, helo-aquatic rescue, and other technical rescue disciplines. NPS maintains preconfigured teams that include personnel and equipment from NPS, the U.S. Fish and Wildlife Service, the U.S. Geological Survey (USGS), the Bureau of Indian Affairs, and other DOI components in planning for ESF-9.

When requested, the U.S. Department of Defense (DoD), through the U.S. Northern Command or the U.S. Pacific command (USPACOM), will coordinate facilities, resources, and special capabilities that conduct and support air, land, and maritime SAR operations according to applicable directives, plans, guidelines, and agreements. Per the NSP, the U.S. Air Force and USPACOM provide resources for the organization and coordination of civil SAR services and operations within their assigned SAR Regions and, when requested, to Federal, State, local, tribal, and territorial authorities.

Explosive Ordnance Disposal (EOD)

EOD involves conducting immediate searches to recognize suspect packages or secondary devices and ensuring their safe disposal. EOD teams require specialized training and equipment and are typically located in jurisdictions with sufficient resources and demand to sustain proficiency, as well as in locations that can best serve regional needs. EOD teams are encouraged through MAAs and task force agreements to take their training, equipment, and experience beyond the borders of their municipalities and jurisdictions. The exchange of information and training concerning improvised explosive devices (IEDs) and WMD among international, public, private, and military communities is recognized as a high priority. Although the majority of EOD teams are comprised of LEA personnel, a portion of the discipline is within fire and emergency services.

Special Weapons and Tactics and Tactical Operations

SWAT and tactical units are comprised of law enforcement personnel engaged in high-risk operations involving critical incidents and hostage rescue operations. Capabilities include hostage rescue, active shooter, high-risk arrest and search warrant service, very important personnel security, and counterterrorism. Additional unit capabilities include tactical medics who provide emergency medical services to the team.

Aviation units within law enforcement conduct aerial patrols of CIKR assets and specific jurisdictional areas within their scope of responsibility. These units utilize highly sophisticated equipment to assist in the apprehension of fleeing suspects, locate missing persons, isolate illegal drug operations, and provide airborne security for National Special Security Events (NSSE).

Aviation Units

Aviation units utilize highly sophisticated equipment to provide rapid egress into areas not accessible or easily accessible to ground-based assets. They also support the ability to identify the scope of an incident, monitor the progression of an incident, or secure against a potential incident that covers great distance.

Aviation units may be found in a variety of communities to support a variety of ESS functions including law enforcement, firefighting, EMS, SAR, and others. For example, aviation units may be used to apprehend fleeing suspects, isolate illegal drug operations, provide airborne security, fight wildland fires, locate missing persons, provide MEDEVAC, and perform various rescue operations. Depending on the use and locality, fire and rescue aviation assets may be owned and operated by Federal, State, local, or private resources.

Public Safety Answering Points

PSAPs typically include one or more 9-1-1 operators and dispatchers, communications equipment, computer terminals, and network servers. The 9-1-1 operator determines the service required and forwards the information for dispatch of the appropriate response units. The key elements of a PSAP include the facilities, personnel, and specialized equipment located within the facility, including commercial telephone links for incoming 9-1-1 calls, computer-aided dispatch, public safety radio, and mobile data communications.

1.1.4 Emergency Services Systems

Emergency preparedness is too complex for a single agency, sector, group, or discipline to manage. Particularly in and around metropolitan areas, integrated systems and regional approaches are common given the high population densities, critical infrastructure, and elevated risks of terrorist attacks. There are two common goals associated with regional public safety efforts: enhanced preparedness and good governance. In addition to enhanced preparedness, regional efforts allow State and local jurisdictions to maximize their resources. For example, regional approaches can promote cost sharing to maximize States' use of funds and capitalize on economies of scale, such as purchasing higher quantities of sophisticated equipment at lower costs.

Additionally, commonly implemented ESS systems, such as MAAs and emergency compacts, are essential to the execution of Federal, State, local, tribal, and territorial response and recovery efforts. Horizontal and localized networks and systems can work more effectively across existing jurisdictional and agency boundaries, respond more flexibly and rapidly to the accelerating pace of problems, and remain more resilient under the threat of multiple hazards. The destruction, degradation, or fraudulent use of these systems could significantly impact the ability of the ESS to respond in a timely and appropriate manner.

Table 1-3: High-priority ESS Systems

ESS CIKR	Definition
Multi-agency Coordination Systems	A combination of facilities (including EOCs), equipment, personnel, procedures, and communications integrated into a common system with responsibility for coordinating and supporting domestic incident management activities.
Mutual-Aid Agreements	As advised by the National Incident Management System (NIMS), many State, local, tribal, and territorial governments and private NGOs enter into MAAs to provide emergency assistance to each other in the event of disasters or emergencies. These agreements, often written in advance, are occasionally arranged verbally after a disaster or emergency occurs. MAAs may either be intra- or inter-state.
Emergency Management Assistance Compact	A Congressionally ratified organization that provides form and structure to interstate mutual aid. Through EMAC, a disaster-impacted State can request and receive assistance from other member States quickly and efficiently, resolving two key issues upfront: liability and reimbursement.
Command-Control-Cyber-Intelligence-Information Technology Systems	Systems utilized by emergency service providers to facilitate multi-incident coordination; public information dissemination; interoperability; personnel/management command pathways; resource acquisition; and emergency services, intelligence, and crisis/consequence communications-sharing networks including emergency alerts and warning systems (e.g., PSAPs, Rescue-21, Homeland Security Advisory System).
Specialized Emergency Response Systems	Systems, including personnel, equipment caches, and facilities at the Federal, State, local, tribal, and territorial levels, all of which provide concise functions for public health and safety as well as national security (e.g., Metropolitan Medical Response System).
Regional Coalitions	Regional partnerships, organizations, and governance bodies that enable CIKR protection coordination among CIKR partners within and across geographical areas as well as planning and program implementation aimed at a common hazard or threat environment. These groupings include public-private partnerships that cross jurisdictional, sector, and international boundaries, and take into account dependencies and interdependencies (e.g., Urban Areas Security Initiative Program).

1.1.5 Interdependencies

Many assets within the ESS depend on multiple elements and systems from other CIKR sectors to maintain functionality. In some cases, a failure in one sector will have a significant impact on the ability of another sector to perform necessary functions. Reliance on another sector is called a dependency. A dependency is a linkage or connection between two infrastructure, through which the state of one infrastructure influences or is correlated to the state of the other. For example, under normal operating conditions, an ESS facility requires electricity, natural gas, and water to function. It requires IT and telecommunications to carry out necessary operations and functions, as well as transportation to move employees to and from the site to continue essential functions. If two assets are dependent on one another, then they are interdependent.

It is extremely important to identify dependencies and interdependencies, both at the sector and asset levels, to comprehend completely the consequences of a successful attack on an asset and to identify the manner in which attacks on other sector assets could impact a dependent or interdependent asset. Today's infrastructure has become so interconnected and interdependent that every action sends ripples throughout multiple domains. Understanding dependencies and interdependencies ensures safe, secure, and resilient infrastructure. Within the ESS, identifying, understanding, and analyzing interdependencies and dependencies create challenges because of the diversity and complexity of assets and of other sectors that are potentially involved.

Internal Interdependencies

In the overall scheme of the ESS, each discipline depends on other disciplines. For example, in many events, law enforcement officers provide protection to fire department and EMS personnel at the scene of an emergency. Similarly, public works personnel may need to clear debris from emergency routes to facilitate access to the site by emergency responders. All ESS sector disciplines rely on emergency managers—regardless of their level of government—for coordination, information, communications, and response and recovery initiatives during large scale and multijurisdictional incidents or terrorist situations. Fundamentally, each ESS discipline relies on various other disciplines to develop associated and interdependent protective strategies, and all disciplines are dependent on other CIKR sectors. The goal of the NIPP sector partnership model and ESS is to establish the context, framework, and support for coordination and information-sharing activities required to implement a full spectrum of prudent and responsible protective strategies across all CIKR sectors in support of the emergency responder.

External Interdependencies

Although the ESS is a primary "protector" of other CIKR sectors, it is also highly impacted by events in the operating environment. Loss or incapacitation of ESS assets, systems, and networks would clearly have a negative impact on the Nation's security, public safety, and morale. A degradation of ESS response capability would negatively impact on a wide range of organizations and communities; all other CIKR sectors; many, if not all ESFs; all Federal departments and agencies; State, local, tribal, and territorial governments; the public sector across industries; and the public at large. The degradation or loss of any of the above organizations, systems, or groups could have a significant negative impact on the ability of the ESS to mobilize, respond, and carry out the mission successfully. Emergency services are most directly dependent on the energy, telecommunications, water and transportation infrastructure, but interdependencies may vary considerably across the disciplines and jurisdictions. Identifying these interdependencies is an important step in developing protective programs and initiatives to improve the security and resilience of the sector.

The importance of ESS interdependencies with each of their disciplines, other CIKR sectors, and public service entities clearly illustrates the significance of partnerships in developing protective strategies for the sector. Fundamentally, each ESS discipline relies on various other disciplines to develop associated and interdependent protective strategies, and all ESS disciplines are dependent on other CIKR sectors.

1.2 Sector Partners

Protecting the assets, systems, and networks of the ESS requires strong collaboration and partnerships among all levels of government, regional organizations, sector owners and operators, and associations that represent disciplines within the sector. Any effective process for securing the ESS infrastructure depends on the collaboration and partnership between a wide range of sector partners. The perspective and expertise of these partners are critical to any framework for identifying ESS CIKR assets, systems, and networks; assessing their vulnerabilities; and developing protective strategies and programs aimed at improving the safety and survivability of the ESS operational elements.

1.2.1 NIPP Partnership Model

The NIPP sector partnership model facilitates coordination between all levels of government and the owners and operators. It encourages formation of Sector Coordinating Councils (SCCs) and Government Coordinating Councils (GCCs), and provides guidance, tools, and support so that these groups can work together to carry out their respective independent and collective protective functions. The protective umbrella of the CIPAC enables the free sharing of CIKR information between government and CIKR owners and operators. The intent is that through partnership, sector partners will be able to collaborate on sensitive security issues in a protected environment that fosters open communication to develop protective programs, plans, and processes designed to secure the sector.

1.2.1.1 Sector-Specific Agency

DHS is the SSA for the ESS. Within DHS, SSA responsibilities are delegated to the Office of Infrastructure Protection (IP). As the SSA, IP has numerous responsibilities including leading, integrating, and coordinating the overall national effort to enhance ESS CIKR protection. Key responsibilities include:

- Identifying, prioritizing, and coordinating protection of sector CIKR, with a particular focus on CIKR that could be exploited to cause catastrophic health effects or mass casualties comparable to those produced by a WMD;

- Collaborating with sector partners, including facilitating information sharing and building CIKR partnerships;

- Working with DHS components to develop, evaluate, validate, or modify sector-specific risk assessment tools;

- Assisting sector partners in their efforts to organize and conduct protection and continuity of operations planning, and to elevate awareness and understanding of threats and vulnerabilities;

- Identifying and promoting effective sector-specific CIKR protection practices and methodologies; and

- Monitoring and reporting on performance measures for sector-level CIKR protection and NIPP implementation activities to enable continuous improvement.

1.2.1.2 Federal Sector Partners (Government Coordinating Council)

The GCC provides effective coordination of security strategies and activities, policy, and communications across the Federal Government, and between the government and sector stakeholders, to support the Nation's homeland security mission.

The GCC consists of members whose departments and agencies are integral to the sector and responsible for coordinating CIKR strategies and activities, policy, and communication within their organizations, across government, and between governments and sector members. The GCC acts as the counterpart and partner to the SCC in planning, implementing, and executing sector-wide infrastructure protection programs.

- **U.S. Department of Homeland Security**

  - **Federal Emergency Management Agency** – FEMA leads the effort to prepare the Nation for all-hazards disasters and effectively manages Federal response and recovery efforts following any national incident.

  - **Immigration and Customs Enforcement** – Immigration and Customs Enforcement (ICE) enforces immigration and customs laws to help protect the United States against terrorist attacks.

  - **Office of Infrastructure Protection** – IP leads the coordinated national effort to reduce the risk to CIKR posed by acts of terrorism, and strengthens preparedness, timely response, and rapid recovery in the event of an attack, natural disaster, or other emergency.

  - **Grants Program Directorate** – The Grants Program Directorate (GPD) provides a broad array of assistance for infrastructure protection through funding, coordinated training, exercises, equipment acquisition, and technical assistance.

  - **Science and Technology** – The Science and Technology (S&T) Directorate's mission is to protect the homeland by providing Federal and local officials with state-of-the-art technology and other resources.

- **U.S. Secret Service** – The mission of the U.S. Secret Service (USSS) is to safeguard the Nation's financial infrastructure and payment systems to preserve the integrity of the economy and to protect national leaders, visiting heads of state and government, and designated sites. As a result, the USSS is the lead agency for all National Special Security Events.

- **U.S. Coast Guard** – USCG is responsible for countering threats to America's coasts, ports, and inland waterways through numerous port security, harbor defense, and coastal warfare operations and exercises.

- **U.S. Fire Administration** – USFA's mission is to reduce life and economic losses due to fire and related emergencies. The EMR-ISAC is a function of USFA.

- **Cybersecurity and Communications** – The Office of Cybersecurity and Communications (CS&C) is responsible for enhancing the security, resilience, and reliability of the Nation's cyber and communications infrastructure. CS&C actively engages the public and private sectors as well as international partners to prepare for, prevent, and respond to catastrophic incidents that could degrade or overwhelm these strategic assets.

- **Office of Health Affairs** – The Office of Health Affairs (OHA) serves as DHS' principal agent for all medical and health matters. Working throughout all levels of government and the private sector, OHA leads the Department's role in developing and supporting a scientifically rigorous, intelligence-based biodefense and health preparedness architecture to ensure the security of our Nation in the face of all hazards.

- **State and Local Law Enforcement** – The Assistant Secretary for State and Local Law Enforcement is designated as the primary official responsible for coordinating Department-wide policies related to the role of State, local, and tribal law enforcement in the prevention of, preparation for, protection against, and response to natural disasters, acts of terrorism, and other manmade disasters within the United States. It also provides the State, tribal, and local law enforcement community with an advocate and point of contact within the DHS Office of Policy as well as authorized liaisons within DHS Operational Components.

- **Office of Emergency Communications** – The Office of Emergency Communications (OEC) was created per title XVII of the Homeland Security Act (as amended, as the U.S. focal point for emergency communications). OEC supports and promotes the ability of emergency responders and government officials to communicate in the event of natural disasters, acts of terrorism, or other manmade disasters, and works to ensure, accelerate, and attain interoperable and operable communications nationwide.

- **Transportation Security Administration** – The Transportation Security Administration (TSA) protects the Nation's transportation systems to ensure freedom of movement for people and commerce.

- **U.S. Department of Health and Human Services**

  - **Office of the Assistant Secretary for Preparedness and Response** – The Office of the Assistant Secretary for Preparedness and Response (ASPR) coordinates inter-agency activities among U.S. Department of Health and Human Services (HHS) agencies; other Federal departments, agencies, and offices; and State and local officials responsible for emergency preparedness and protection of the civilian population from bioterrorism and other public health emergencies. HHS is represented by the Healthcare and Public Health SSA.

  - **Indian Health Services** – The Indian Health Services mission is to raise the physical, mental, social, and spiritual health of American Indians and Alaska Natives to the highest level. The future of Indian health care requires coordinated intervention of health care services, educational systems, and economic development programs. Critical to this effort are collaborations and partnerships among tribal nations, urban Indian health organizations, academic medical centers, foundations, businesses, professional organizations, and Federal agencies and programs.

- **U.S. Department of Transportation**

  - **National Highway Traffic Safety Administration/Office of Emergency Medical Systems** – The Office of Emergency Medical Systems within the U.S. Department of Transportation's (DOT) National Highway Traffic Safety Administration (NHTSA) is dedicated to reducing death and disability from motor vehicle crashes and other health emergencies by providing national leadership and coordination of comprehensive, data-driven, and evidence-based emergency medical services and 9-1-1 systems.

- **Environmental Protection Agency**

  - **The Office of Emergency Management** – The Office of Emergency Management (OEM) offers technical assistance to prevent and prepare for chemical emergencies, responds to environmental crises, informs the public about chemical hazards in their communities, and shares lessons learned about chemical accidents. OEM also coordinates and implements a wide range of activities to ensure that adequate and timely response occurs in communities affected by hazardous substances and oil releases where State and local first-responder capabilities have been exceeded or where additional support is needed.

- **U.S. Department of Justice**

  - **Federal Bureau of Investigation** – The Federal Bureau of Investigation (FBI) upholds the law through investigation of violations of Federal criminal law; protects the United States from foreign intelligence and terrorist activities; and provides leadership and law enforcement assistance to Federal, State, local, tribal, territorial, and international agencies.

- **U.S. Department of Defense**

  - **National Guard** – The National Guard of the United States is a reserve military force comprised of State National Guard militia members or units. In peacetime, or to support the governor during times of local emergencies (e.g., blizzard, flooding), the National Guard is commanded by the governor of each respective State or Territory. When ordered to active duty for Federal mobilization or called into Federal service for emergencies, units of the Guard are under the control of the appropriate service secretary. The mission of the National Guard is to maintain properly trained and equipped units available for prompt mobilization for war, national emergency, or as otherwise needed.

- **U.S. Department of Agriculture**

  - **U.S. Forest Service** – Within the U.S. Department of Agriculture (USDA), the Fire & Aviation Management part of the U.S. Forest Service (USFS) provides fire protection on National Forest Lands and supports other Federal, State, and local wildland firefighting agencies with wildland fire and all-hazard response and incident management. USFS works to advance technologies in fire management and suppression, maintain and improve the extremely efficient mobilization and tracking systems in place, and reach out in support of Federal, State, and international fire partners. USFS is also the Coordinator and Primary Agency for ESF-4, Firefighting, under the National Response Framework, and serves as the link between the Federal wildland fire community, DHS/FEMA, and other Federal agencies for issues related to natural and manmade disasters and emergencies.

- **American Red Cross** – In addition to domestic disaster relief, the American Red Cross offers community services that help the needy; support and comfort for military members and their families; collection, processing, and distribution of life-saving blood and blood products; educational programs that promote health and safety; and international relief and development programs.

- **State, Local, Tribal and Territorial Government Coordinating Council** – The State, Local, Tribal, and Territorial Government Coordinating Council (SLTTGCC) serves as a forum to ensure that homeland security advisors or their designated representatives from these jurisdictions are fully integrated as active participants in national CIKR protection efforts. Moreover, the SLTTGCC provides an organizational structure to coordinate across jurisdictions on State and local-level CIKR protection guidance, strategies, and programs.

1.2.1.3 Owner/Operator Sector Partners (Sector Coordinating Council)

The ES Sector Coordinating Council (ES SCC) is a self-organized, self-led body of ESS members who work collaboratively with the SSA, GCC, and EMR-ISAC in developing the entire range of infrastructure protection issues and activities. Such activities include sector-wide planning, development of sector best practices, sector-wide promulgation of programs and plans, development of requirements for effective information sharing, research and development (R&D), and cross-sector coordination.

The ES SCC is organized through professional associations and associate members representing the various types of emergency service providers. Organizing through associations provides consistent representation of the sector, and supports a unified, interdisciplinary approach. Associations can support dissemination of information to hundreds of thousands of emergency service workers; information gathering from national and international emergency service workers; and facilitation of sector collaboration and cross-sector outreach. In addition, associations are able to identify and leverage existing programs and best practices in the field to avoid duplicative programs.

The SCC provides a venue for sector stakeholders to contribute their technical expertise. Each member of the ES SCC is expected not only to represent their discipline or function, but to serve the sector as a whole. The ES SCC provides DHS with a reliable and efficient way to communicate and consult with the sector on protective programs and sector security issues. The members include associations that represent particular entities within the emergency response community and individual practitioners representing their area of expertise. Association members include:

- National Sheriffs' Association
- International Association of Chiefs of Police
- International Association of Emergency Managers
- International Association of Fire Chiefs
- National Association of State EMS Officials
- National Emergency Management Association
- Security Industry Association
- American Ambulance Association
- American Public Works Association
- Central Station Alarm Association
- National Association of Security Companies
- National Association of State Fire Marshals
- National Native American Law Enforcement Association

1.2.1.4 Other CIKR Partners

State, Local, Tribal, and Territorial CIKR Partners

Developing security plans and programs for the ESS requires careful collaboration among all partners, including Federal, State, local, tribal, and territorial governments and the private sector. The ESS is a complicated and interconnected web of these CIKR partners. Each partner has different, often overlapping responsibilities within the sector. Responsibility for incident management initially falls on State, local, tribal, and territorial authorities, but the majority of ESS disciplines are organized and provided at the local level of government by career and volunteer personnel from the communities.

The SSA, GCC, and SCC coordinate with State, local, tribal, and territorial CIKR partners as needed to ensure protective programs and initiatives are developed in an executable and coordinated fashion across all areas of the Emergency Services community. One of the primary methods of coordination is through the SLTTGCC. The SLTTGCC strengthens the sector partnership by providing policy and strategic guidance to State, local, tribal, and territorial governments related to the CIKR protection process. Members of the SLTTGCC are geographically diverse and offer broad institutional knowledge from a wide range of professional disciplines that relate to CIKR protection.

Regional Coordination

Regional CIKR partnerships involve multijurisdictional, cross-sector, and public-private sector efforts focused on the preparedness, protection, response, and recovery of infrastructure and the associated economies within a defined population or geographic area. Because of the specific challenges and interdependencies facing individual regions and the broad range of public and private sector partners, regional efforts are often complex and diverse.

The SSA, GCC, and SCC collaborate with regional coordination groups as needed to ensure a coordinated and robust path forward for ESS security. One such group includes the Regional Consortium Coordinating Council (RCCC), formed by DHS in July 2008. Members of the RCCC include regionally significant organizations that work toward infrastructure protection and resilience within their respective mission areas. This may include enhancing physical, cyber, and personnel security of infrastructure, emergency preparedness, and overall industrial and governmental continuity and resilience of one or more States, urban areas, or municipalities.

As appropriate, the ESS coordinates with Local Emergency Planning Committees (LEPCs). LEPCs were established by the Emergency Planning and Community Right-to-Know Act (EPCRA), which includes emergency planning and community right-to-know requirements. The LEPC is responsible for the development, training, and testing of the community's hazardous substances emergency response plan; development of procedures for regulated facilities to provide information and emergency notification to the LEPCs; and development of procedures for receiving and processing requests from the public under EPCRA. A major role for the LEPC is to work with industry and the interested public to encourage continuous attention to chemical safety, risk reduction, and accident prevention by each local stakeholder. Examples of additional coordinating councils include the FEMA Regional Coordinating Councils, Urban Areas Security Initiative Regions, and Metropolitan Medical Response System entities.

Advisory Councils and Committees

InterAgency Board - The InterAgency Board (IAB) is comprised of practitioners across the range of ESS disciplines that provide invaluable consultative support to the ESS and work collaboratively with the sector to avoid duplication of effort among Federal and State agencies. The IAB is organized around seven subgroups, which include: Standards Coordination, Science and Technology, Equipment, Best Practices, Information Management and Communications Subgroup, Training and Exercises, Health, Medical & Responder Safety.

National Homeland Security Consortium - The National Homeland Security Consortium is a group of key State and local organizations, elected officials, private sector representatives, and others with roles and responsibilities for homeland security prevention, preparedness, and response and recovery activities. It provides a forum of key national organizations to foster effective communication, collaboration, and coordination that positively promotes national policies, strategies, practices, and guidelines to preserve the public health, safety, and security of the Nation.

1.3 Sector Goals and Objectives

Supporting the overarching goal of the NIPP requires a coordinated approach for protective activities across the sector. Sector goals encompass the goals laid out by HSPD-7 for all Federal departments and agencies with regard to infrastructure protection, as well as goals developed specifically for the ESS. The sector vision statement provides the framework to direct its overarching risk management focus and strategy.

1.3.1 Emergency Services Sector Vision Statement

The ESS Vision Statement serves as a description of the desired end-state protective posture that contributes to a coordinated direction for protective activities across the sector.

Vision Statement for the Emergency Services Sector

An Emergency Services Sector in which facilities, key support systems, information and coordination systems, and personnel are protected from both ordinary operational risks and from extraordinary risks or attacks, ensuring timely, coordinated all-hazards emergency response and public confidence in the sector.

1.3.2 Sector Goals

The SSA collaborates with sector partners to create goals that represent the sector's view of how best to support the overarching goal of the NIPP and to achieve a secure, protected, and resilient ESS. These goals underline the sector's emphasis on protecting the human as well as physical assets of the sector. The following goals emphasize collaboration among all the sector partners, including an engaged sector community that is well-informed and takes responsibility for its own safety and sustainability. These goals provide the framework for enduring capabilities that serve the sector's preparedness and protective needs over the long term, which promotes sustainability and resilience. From these goals and specific objectives, milestones are developed which allow progress toward the sector's vision to be measured. The CIKR protection goals for the ESS are:

1. Partnership Engagement
2. Situational Awareness
3. Prevention, Preparedness, and Protection
4. Sustainability, Resilience, and Reconstitution

Goal 1: Partnership Engagement

To build a partnership model that enables the sector to effectively sustain a collaborative planning and decision-making culture. The objectives for Goal 1 are to:

- Strengthen regional approaches to CIKR protective planning and decision making;

- Utilize sector–wide processes to identify and close gaps through development of protective programs;

- Develop and refine processes and mechanisms for ongoing coordination and collaboration, including majority sector participation on councils and working groups that support development and implementation of protective programs;

- Coordinate the identification of research and development (R&D) priorities for the ESS, and the pursuit of creative, affordable methods and tools for performing sector CIKR protection activities; and

- Provide the platform to reduce redundancy and duplicative efforts by both public and private entities within the sector.

Goal 2: Situational Awareness

To support an information-sharing environment that ensures the availability and flow of accurate, timely, and relevant CIKR information and intelligence about terrorist threats and other hazards, information analysis, and incident reporting. The objectives for Goal 2 are to:

- Collaborate, develop, and share appropriate threat and vulnerability information among public and private sector partners;

- Expand strategic analytical capabilities that facilitate public and private sector partner collaboration to identify potential incidents;

- Compile and disseminate best protective practices and lessons learned materials related to development and implementation of protective measures or activities, including cost-benefit analyses;

- Increase awareness of cybersecurity issues impacting ESS infrastructure to encourage sharing and implementation of cybersecurity programs; and

- Report on CIKR protection effectiveness to relevant sector partners throughout the Federal, State, and local governments, as well as the private sector.

Goal 3: Prevention, Preparedness, and Protection

To employ a risk-based approach to developing protective efforts designed to improve the overall posture of the sector through targeted risk management decisions and initiatives. The objectives for Goal 3 are to:

- Update prioritization of critical assets within the ESS on an ongoing basis as determined by the general threat environment and the associated risk, both of which allow for comparison of risks associated with ESS assets to assets in other CIKR sectors. Assess and prioritize risks to critical ESS functions, including evaluating emerging threats, vulnerabilities, and cybersecurity, and mapping them against the infrastructure to prioritize efforts;

- Tailor protective measures to mitigate associated consequences, vulnerabilities, and threats, to accommodate the diversity of the ESS;

- Develop and share ESS model practices and protective measures with sector partners; and

- Develop metrics to measure effectiveness of sector CIKR protection efforts and develop a means of gathering the information needed to measure effectiveness that is not unduly burdensome on asset owners and operators or other sector partners.

Goal 4: Sustainability, Resilience, and Reconstitution

To improve the sustainability and resilience of the sector and increase the speed and efficiency of restoration of normal services, levels of security, and economic activity following an incident. The objectives of Goal 4 are to:

- Strengthen all components of an integrated region-wide response and recovery capability;

- Enhance the ability of Federal, State, local, tribal, and territorial governments and the private sector to respond effectively to emergencies resulting from a terrorist attack, natural disaster, or other incidents; and

- Improve and expand effective resource-sharing systems and standards.

1.3.4 Process to Establish Sector Goals

The sector created the ESS goals through a facilitated discussion, and they represent its view of how best to support the overarching goal of the NIPP. The NIPP framework and sector-level goals provide the common vision necessary to achieve CIKR protection in the sector. With this vision in mind, sector CIKR partners can best determine the specific risk-reduction and protective strategies that will best enhance security, and define measures to evaluate progress to achieve that end. Effective ESS protection partnerships must be built on trusted relationships based on the foundation of common vision, goals, and objectives shared by public and private sector CIKR partners. To develop a common vision and supporting goals to achieve a secure, protected, and resilient ESS requires that the vision and goals be based on an agreed-on end state that represents a desirable protective posture. Each partner has unique assets, operational processes, business environments, and risk management approaches. The sector goals reflect the overall risk management outcomes that the CIKR partners seek to achieve.

1.4 Value Proposition

The full engagement of ESS partners in developing and implementing protective programs depends on understanding the benefits through participation in the partnership model. The sector partnership model provides an opportunity to work collaboratively to:

- **Improve Access to Threat Information:** DHS and the ES SSA work to ensure the timely and appropriate sharing of threat information with ESS partners to enable proper protection of the ESS critical infrastructure.

- **Improve Information Sharing:** Participation in the sector partnership enables information sharing and connections with ongoing initiatives, both public and private, through a collaborative forum designed to raise awareness and increase security.

- **Impact National Policy and Procedure:** Through participation in the GCC or SCC, organizations and individuals have the opportunity to leverage their expertise to make substantive changes to national policy that reflect the role of ESS as a CIKR partner in homeland security.

- **Enhance Research and Development Support:** DHS and the ES SSA incorporate input from sector partners to help inform the sector and therefore assist in the prioritization of R&D projects which may touch directly and indirectly on the activities of ES personnel.

- **Focus CIKR Protection Activities:** The ES SSA and its sector partners participate in the development of realistic and sustainable protective measures and strategies that work at the jurisdictional or discipline level and are designed to better inform resource allocation.

- **Increase Sector Resilience:** Participation in the sector partnership enables the development of a comprehensive protective strategy to increase ESS resilience and security.

All ESS partners are urged to participate in sector efforts, communicate CIKR protection activities to appropriate representatives, and express their concerns to sector leaders who can advise them of appropriate channels to follow for problem resolution. By these means, the overall protective posture of the ESS and the Nation's infrastructure security will be improved.

2. Identify Assets, Systems, and Networks

The ESS is focused on developing all-hazards protective programs for physical, cyber, and human critical infrastructure to ensure that it can securely and effectively perform its mission to save lives, protect property and the environment, provide disaster assistance, and recover from emergency situations. To manage critical infrastructure protection activities and resources effectively, the ESS must be able to identify those assets, systems, and networks that comprise the sector. This chapter describes the process that the sector will use to identify and gather, validate, and update pertinent information on the assets, systems, and networks within the sector (see Figure 2-1).

Figure 2-1: NIPP Risk Management Framework: Identify Assets, Systems, and Networks

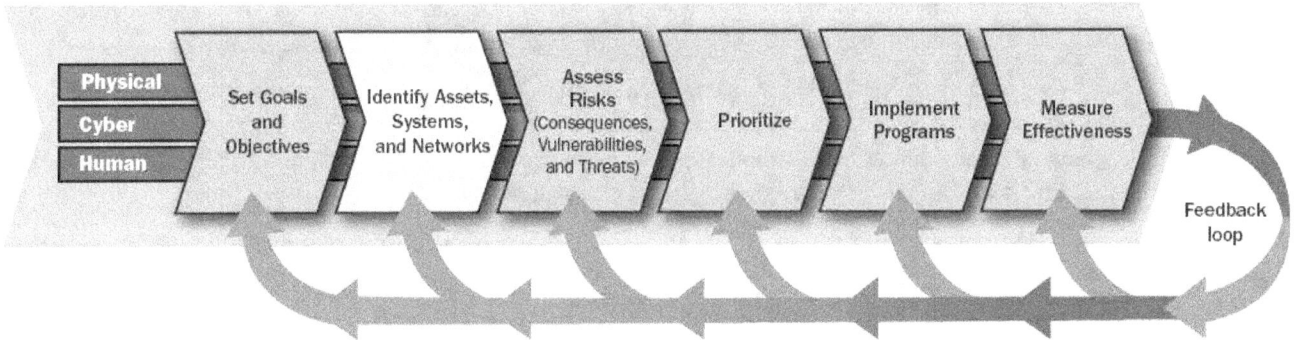

Continuous Improvement to enhance protection of CIKR

2.1 Defining Information Parameters

As discussed in chapter 1, the ESS has defined itself along five broad disciplines: 1) Law Enforcement, 2) Fire and Emergency Services, 3) Emergency Medical Services, 4) Emergency Management, and 5) Public Works. Supplementing these disciplines and overall sector operations are specialized capabilities specific to the ESS: HAZMAT, SAR, EOD, SWAT, Aviation Units, and PSAPs. The human, physical, and cyber critical infrastructure that support and comprise each ESS discipline and specialized capabilities define the parameters for information collection and infrastructure identification.

The ESS will draw on numerous existing and emerging information sources and databases to identify CIKR and collect information. The Target Capabilities List (TCL) is one source for guiding the sector's strategic direction of information collection efforts. The TCL describes the collective national capabilities required to prevent, protect against, respond to, and recover from terrorist attacks, major disasters, and other emergencies. By leveraging TCL information, the ESS can identify the critical infrastructure required to support core sector capabilities and develop programs to enhance the protection of the sector's people, equipment, and systems responsible for maintaining those capabilities. This will ensure a secure, resilient, and effective emergency services infrastructure.

2.1.1 Emergency Services Sector Information Parameters

The ESS consists of assets, systems, and networks that perform preparedness, prevention, response, and recovery missions. These elements are critical to protecting communities, property, and the environment; saving lives; and recovering essential services. The key is to identify the specific components that, in their incapacitation or destruction, would result in a debilitating impact on the Nation's security, national economic security, national public health and safety, or public confidence. ESS assets, systems, and networks include physical, cyber, and human elements. Each of these elements contains a variety of specific components that contribute to the protection of the sector, as detailed below:

Physical CIKR Elements

Physical CIKR elements include equipment and materials, facilities, conveyances, and records that support or provide protection for the ESS. Examples include:

- *Equipment and Materials:* Unique devices, parts, or pieces of equipment (e.g., Personal Protective Equipment, such as HAZMAT protective gear, respirators, crowd control equipment), including key elements of communications systems (e.g., radios);

- *Facilities:* Physical structures that house or directly support ESS personnel, equipment, conveyances, records, and cyber elements. Examples of ESS facilities include fire stations, police stations, training facilities, crime labs, and SAR stations;

  – *Communications Facilities:* Communications infrastructure (e.g., PSAPs (9-1-1 call centers), EOCs) used by ESS providers to enable effective steady-state and incident communications, information exchange, and interoperability;

- *Conveyances:* Vehicles used to carry out critical ESS missions. Examples include vehicles used in emergency response (e.g., fire engines, ambulances, police cars), mobile command centers, marine vessels, aircraft, and other vehicles used in specialized activities. For common ESS conveyances, information is defined by asset class, rather than by individual asset (e.g., the number of police squad cars in a given region, rather than an individual police car); and

- *Records:* Documents in electronic or non-electronic media, including sensitive or classified government information, personnel records, accountability records, equipment inventory, financial information, and personally identifiable information.

Cyber CIKR Elements

Cyber CIKR elements include hardware and software components that are critical to supporting ESS missions, including computers, servers, databases, and other IT systems and assets used in ESS activities. Cyber CIKR may be identified individually or included as a cyber element of a facility or asset, system, or network, and typically fulfill one of four roles:

1. *Access Control* limits physical access to defined areas of a facility to authorized personnel and visitors only.

2. *Control Systems* are used to monitor and control sensitive processes and physical functions (most communications systems fall within this role).

3. *Warning and Alert* functions are used for alerting and notification purposes to pass critical information that triggers protection and response actions.

4. *Data Collection Systems* are used in the collection of data by personnel.

Human elements of the ESS include personnel who have unique training, certification, knowledge, skills, authorities, or roles, and whose absence could cause undesirable consequences or hamper the sector's mission. In general, the human aspect is best captured within the system dimension of the assets, systems, and networks continuum. Categories of positions that support continuity of operations at all levels of government and functioning of the ESS include:

- *Strategic Positions:* Individuals who must be identified, assessed, and prioritized for protection to ensure continuity of essential government operations. Often, such positions include the leadership of the ESS and those whose functions are critical to enabling the sector to maintain a specific capability at acceptable effectiveness levels;

- *Operational Positions:* Individuals responsible for operating CIKR systems, which, if impaired could result in either cessation or takeover of operations, or if compromised would make recovery from an attack more difficult (e.g., HAZMAT experts, individual responders, bomb squad members);

- *Specialized Response Units:* Personnel teams trained to carry out specific emergency response missions. Examples include bomb squads; crime scene investigation units; K-9 units; SWAT teams; Federal law enforcement response units; specially trained medical personnel, such as Disaster Medical Assistance Teams (DMATs); HAZMAT units; Chemical, Biological, Radiological, Nuclear, and high-yield Explosives (CBRNE) response units; marine rescue and fireboat units; air rescue units; and SAR units, including Structure Collapsed (Urban) SAR, Maritime/Coastal/Waterborne SAR, and Land SAR; and

- *Mutual-Aid and Multi-Agency Coordination:* Formal and informal agreements and processes designed to connect agencies in different jurisdictions and enable a coordinated response to emergencies.

Currently, DHS IP maintains a national inventory of ESS assets, systems, and networks. This database maintains the information to help inform steady-state CIKR protection approaches, and inform and support the response to a wide array of incidents and emergencies. The database information comes from current sources, such as sector inventories; IP's Infrastructure Information Collection Division (IICD) database inventory; voluntary submissions from CIKR partners; and periodic data calls. For example, IP's Office for Bombing Prevention (OBP) uses a tool, the National Capabilities Analysis Database (NCAD), to set and measure progress toward preparedness goals, as well as to provide reports on response assets and to visually model threats, vulnerabilities, and response capabilities within a given jurisdiction or region. The ES SSA, GCC, and SCC will work with other sector partners to ensure the information is accurate, current, and secure.

As critical ESS assets, systems, and networks are identified, the information gathered by the sector will include data such as the following elements:

- Type of asset (such as facilities, equipment, class of vehicles, communications);

- Owners and operators (including name, location, phone number, and point of contact);

- Location of fixed assets and geographic territory information for mobile assets;

- Inventories of personnel components or critical components of a system;

- Presence or absence of internal and external resource redundancy;

- Systems or key capabilities supported (e.g., HAZMAT response);

- Existing protective measures and shortfalls; and

- Critical dependencies and interdependencies related to external sectors (e.g., energy and water sources).

2.2 Collecting Infrastructure Information

A variety of information sources and databases exist, many of which address portions of the possible data fields required. The ESS works with the GCC and SCC to review current methods of data collection and to identify and discuss other potential means for data collection that may be more efficient or encompassing, or less expensive than current data collection methods. Information sources include existing DHS tools, as well as databases at the State and local level. Examples of existing DHS databases include the following:

- *National Capabilities Asset Database:* a database developed by OBP, in partnership with the Homeland Security Council Improvised Explosive Device Working Group. The program generates data that are being accumulated and analyzed to determine overall national bombing prevention capabilities. The data come from the hundreds of bomb squads serving communities across the country.

- *Automated Critical Asset Management System (ACAMS):* a secure, Web-based information services portal used to support infrastructure protection efforts at the State and local level. It focuses on pre-incident prevention and protection and assists in post-incident response. It also allows users to manage the collection and effective use of CIKR asset data.

- *Homeland Infrastructure Foundation-Level Data (HIFLD):* a database promoting domestic infrastructure geospatial information gathering, sharing, visualization, and spatial knowledge management.

- *Homeland Security Infrastructure Protection (HSIP) Gold:* a unified homeland infrastructure foundational geospatial data inventory assembled by the National Geospatial-Intelligence Agency (NGA) in partnership with the DoD, DHS, and USGS for use in homeland defense and homeland security communities. It is the compilation of best available Federal Government and commercial proprietary data sets.

- *Linking Encrypted Network System (LENS):* a system that captures data from Site Assistance Visits, Buffer Zone Protection Plans, Comprehensive Reviews, and Enhanced Critical Infrastructure Protection (ECIP) assessment visits. The DHS Protective Security Coordination Division leads LENS in conjunction with subject matter experts and local law enforcement personnel to assist sector partners assess and characterize vulnerabilities at their critical infrastructure sites.

- *Target Capabilities List (TCL):* a list that defines 37 specific capabilities that communities, the private sector, and all levels of government should collectively possess in order to prepare for, protect from, respond to, and recover from disasters effectively. The TCL is mapped against the 15 National Planning Scenarios, which are planning tools that represent a minimum number of credible scenarios depicting the range of potential terrorist attacks and natural disasters and related impacts facing our Nation. They form a basis for coordinated Federal planning, training, and exercises. The TCL will serve as a valuable guide for ESS capabilities-based assessments and a solid foundation from which to identify critical assets, systems, and networks.

The principal national inventory of CIKR assets and systems is the Infrastructure Data Warehouse (IDW). The IDW comprises a federated data architecture that provides a single virtual view of one or more infrastructure data sources. DHS uses these data to provide all relevant public and private sector CIKR partners with access to the most current and comprehensive view of the Nation's infrastructure information allowed under applicable Federal, State, or local regulation.

Currently, the Infrastructure Information Collection System (IICS) maintains the inventory and its associated attributes. IICS is a federated IDW, accessible through the capabilities provided by the Integrated Common Analytical Viewer (iCAV) suite of tools, including iCAV and DHS Earth, or through a tool adapted, modified, or developed specifically for the sector. Critical infrastructure information submitted to DHS is considered sensitive and proprietary and is protected from public disclosure to the maximum extent permitted by law.

2.3 Verifying Infrastructure Information

Given the breadth of the sector and the variety of information sources and databases containing information on ESS assets, systems, and networks, the SSA is reliant on the owners of the sources and databases from which the information is gathered. Additionally, procedures for submission and verification of infrastructure information vary considerably depending on the database or specific program involved. Many databases and information sources may already have robust verification procedures in place. The SSA will work with sector partners, including the GCC and SCC, as well as the owners of information sources, to develop procedures for verifying ESS infrastructure information. By leveraging the expertise and support of sector partners, the SSA will supplement all existing verification efforts to ensure infrastructure information remains accurate and complete.

2.4 Updating Infrastructure Information

The ESS recognizes the importance of regularly updating infrastructure information to ensure the development of accurate and effective risk mitigation measures. However, as with verification, the wide variety of ESS infrastructure information sources presents challenges to updating this information. No single procedure exists for updating ESS information that encompasses each of the information sources. Recognizing these challenges, the SSA will work with sector partners, including the SCC and GCC, to determine the appropriate mechanism to update infrastructure information for the various databases in use. Where existing mechanisms are unable to adequately update database information, the SSA will work to develop alternative methods to ensure updated information is submitted in a consistent manner. These methods will be tailored to the needs of the sector and are dependent on the availability of the resources necessary to provide updates.

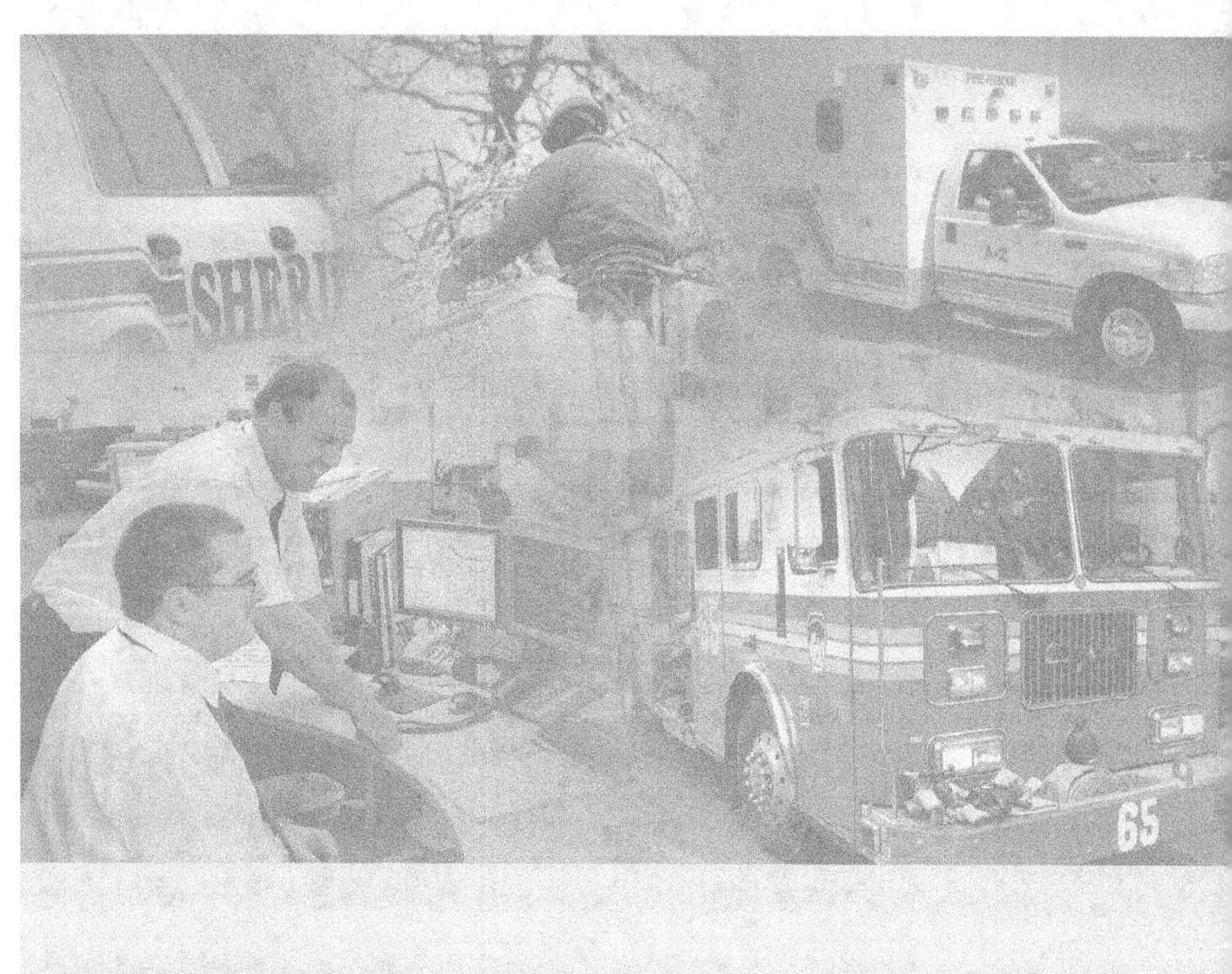

3. Assess Risks (Consequences, Vulnerabilities, and Threats)

The ESS is comprised of assets, systems, and networks that encompass the physical, cyber, and human components of CIKR for ESS. When considering sector risk, there are three general risk assessment layers, listed in increasing complexity: (1) facility-specific or fixed assets, (2) specialized emergency services assets or systems, and (3) multiple systems in a region or multiple regions. At the simplest layer, the risk to a particular fixed asset is evaluated based on pre-defined risk attributes. Multiple fixed assets, as well as specialized equipment and trained personnel comprise the systems that represent the next layer; multiple systems considered together represent the most complex layer, the regional or multi-regional system. The risk attributes specific to each layer build on those of the previous layer to develop the overall regional risk perspective.

This layered approach for assessing risk utilizes an existing vulnerability-assessment framework and builds on it by enhancing and customizing the vulnerability component, and adding sector-specific threat and consequence components. The resulting Emergency Services Self Assessment Tool (ESSAT) enables government and public and private entities to perform risk assessments of fixed assets, systems, regional systems, and critical assets. The tool encourages voluntary and interactive stakeholder involvement and allows for a coordinated effort among sector partners by collecting and sharing common risk gaps, obstacles, and protective measures. The tool benefits both individual partners and collective disciplines and supports sector-wide risk management efforts.

Figure 3-1: Assess Risks (Consequences, Vulnerabilities, and Threats)

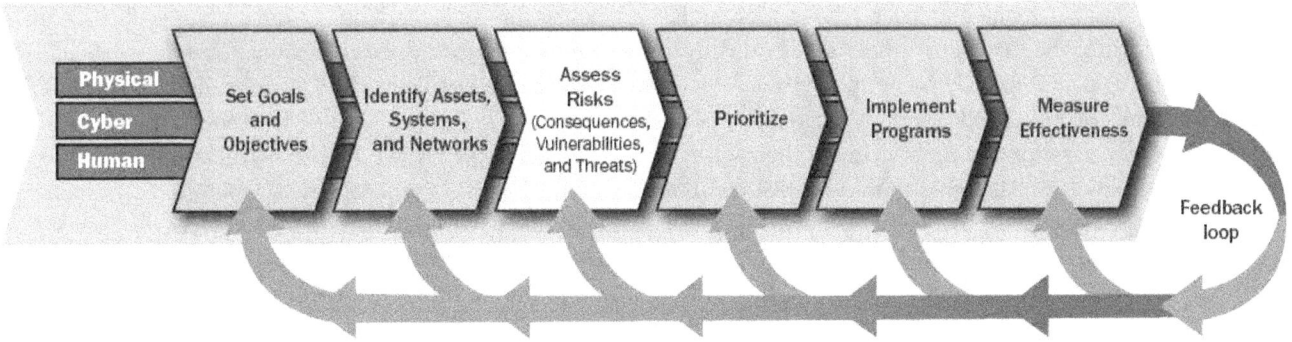

Continuous Improvement to enhance protection of CIKR

Currently, IP's Protective Security Advisors (PSAs) conduct ECIP assessments at select ESS locations. Since 2003, PSAs have assessed vulnerabilities of 18 Emergency Services facilities. The ECIP assessment is designed to assess overall site security, identify gaps, recommend protective measures, educate facility owners and operators on security, and promote communication and information sharing among facility owners and operators, DHS, and State governments. Information collected during ECIP visits is used to develop ECIP metrics; conduct sector and cross-sector vulnerability comparisons; identify security gaps and trends; establish baseline security survey scores for the sector; and track progress toward improving CIKR facility protection through activities, programs, outreach, and training.

Although the ECIP assessment produces invaluable vulnerability information collected by the PSAs and provided to the facilities, the sector suggested the establishment of a Risk Assessment Working Group (RAWG) to further examine the ECIP and discuss risk assessments of critical elements in the ESS and its subcomponents. A Risk Assessment Workshop was conducted in July 2009, where 22 practitioners from across the country, representing a majority of the ESS disciplines, established the RAWG.

The RAWG, comprised of workshop participants and SCC and GCC representation, currently leads the effort to enhance the ECIP vulnerability assessment. The assessment of fixed assets represents the foundational layer of risk assessment for ESS. Once the risk assessment methodology for this layer is complete, development of the methodology for assessing risk at the systems layer and eventually at the regional layer will begin. The process continues to build until all three layers are incorporated.

The cornerstone of the NIPP is its risk analysis and management framework that establishes the processes for combining consequence, vulnerability, and threat information to produce assessments of national or sector risk. The limited threat component of the ECIP requires expansion to create an adjustable threat module that is appropriate for each particular assessed asset (e.g., if no hurricanes occur in a given geographical location, then hurricanes would not be part of the threat profile for that asset). Section 3.5: Assessing Threat will further explain threat profiles. The consequence component, which has yet to be developed, is the third component of the NIPP risk assessment calculation formula, thus creating a full NIPP-founded risk methodology. The sector will base this module on identifying consequences that are adjustable and appropriate for the assessed asset (e.g., consequences that may be determined by the amount of time it takes for backup units to respond in the absence or delay of the assessed unit).

The ESSAT is envisioned to be the final product that can be used by emergency managers, specialty unit leaders, and regional response and planning personnel. When completed, the ESSAT will enable the sector to select and define a region's area of response parameters, threat profile, and consequence profile to assess risk in one or more facility-specific or fixed assets, specialized emergency services assets or systems, and multiple systems in a region or multiple regions. The ESSAT will use existing and emerging data sets as they become available and are located in IP's IICS and the IDW.

Emergency responders view their risk from an all-hazards perspective, and thus, any type of incident, whether manmade or natural, poses great risk to the responder. However, given the sector's structure and composition, some very specific risks are of greater concern to the sector than others, specifically the intentional release of contagious human diseases and cyber attacks. Strategic targeting of cyber attacks on business systems, such as the Computer-Aided Dispatch (CAD) systems for Public Safety Answering Points (PSAPs), would seriously impede the sector's ability to react and respond swiftly to incidents, as these systems are necessary for the sector to communicate and transmit accurate information. As a result, the sector's initial approach will focus on these threats. For the cyber component, ESS collaborates with the National Cyber Security Division (NCSD) to conduct a cyber risk assessment of selected PSAP assets, which it will incorporate into the overall risk assessment process for the ESS. NCSD is DHS' lead for securing cyberspace and our Nation's cyber assets and networks.

Figure 3-2 shows a visual representation of the NIPP risk assessment calculation formula. The following sections describe the three components of risk and more detailed aspects of each to be used by the sector in the development of a comprehensive risk assessment.

Figure 3-2: Calculating Risk

Risk (R) = f (Consequences (C), Vulnerability (V), Threat (T))

3.1 Use of Risk Assessment in the Sector

Currently, risk assessment for ESS assets is used primarily at the local level (i.e., facility and emergency manager) on fixed assets. The following six distinguishing characteristics represent important factors for consideration in addressing risk assessment efforts of the sector:

The most critical feature of the ESS is its large, geographically distributed base of facilities, equipment, and highly skilled personnel who provide services in both career and volunteer capacities.

The sector is largely organized at the State, local, tribal, and territorial levels of government. Because of its complex and dispersed nature, an adversary would have a difficult time disabling the entire system. Moreover, the sector's inherent diversity also presents challenges in coordinating emergency responses across disciplines, regions, and levels of government.

The sector relies heavily on complex communication and IT systems to enable robust communications and appropriate coordination and management of diverse elements during emergencies.

Specialized transportation vehicles and secure transportation routes are utilized to facilitate sector operations because personnel, equipment, critical resources, and victims must be moved to and from scenes of emergencies.

Interdependencies and dependencies exist with multiple CIKR sectors that supply essential operational elements (e.g., Energy, IT, Water), as well as the National Response Framework's Emergency Support Functions needed by emergency responders themselves (e.g., Public Works and Engineering, Health and Medical Services).

The focus of the sector is primarily on its response mission rather than protecting the sector itself, which presents unique challenges in addressing the protection of ES as a CIKR sector.

The sector is eager to expand into the second and third layers (system and regional) of risk assessment, which are the most difficult layers to develop. As stated above, the fixed assets are not the primary concern of the sector, although they are the building block to capture the systems and regional aspects of ESS risk assessment. A visualization and geospatial capability incorporated into the ESSAT will allow users to map their assets, identify service areas of responsibility, and obtain high-level specialty capability information, including dependencies. As ESSAT matures, its use will expand for regional and national levels.

3.2 Screening Infrastructure

The ability to screen infrastructure depends on a well-defined and mature risk management process. Currently, the ESS is still working to develop its approach to assessing risk within the sector and is limited in its ability to screen infrastructure effectively. Therefore, all of the sector's assets will "screen in." Until the sector has defined its risk management process, ESS relies on the HITRAC National Critical Infrastructure Prioritization Program to nominate critical ESS assets, systems, and networks. Practitioner representation from each discipline participated in the following programs to nominate critical ESS assets for the sector.

The Risk Integration and Analysis Branch (RIAB), within DHS IP HITRAC, performs infrastructure-related decision-support analysis and prioritization for Federal, State, local, tribal, territorial, and private sector partners through the following four major program areas:

- National Critical Infrastructure Prioritization Program (NCIPP), including the Level 1/Level 2 Program and Critical Foreign Dependencies Initiative;

- National Infrastructure Risk Analysis Program, including the Strategic Homeland Infrastructure Risk Analysis process;

- Infrastructure Risk Analysis Partnership Program; and

- Critical Infrastructure Futures Analysis Program.

3.3 Assessing Consequences

DHS defines consequence as the effect of an event, incident, or occurrence that reflects the level, duration, and nature of the loss resulting from the incident. It is commonly considered to include the following four components: public health and safety, economic, psychological, and governance or mission impact. Consequence factors are yet to be determined by the sector; however, the following discussion points should be considered in the development of the consequence component of the ESSAT:

- **Public Health and Safety** – refers to the effect on human life and physical well-being (e.g., fatalities, injury, or illness). The human component for ESSAT may encompass the population density of the area of the emergency responders for the facility or response capability for conducting the assessment. This may be different for the various types of hazard situations. Generally, this component is measured by the number of lives affected or population at risk. It can also incorporate a unit of time during which the event negatively impacts the element or region (e.g., delays in response capacity or delivery of goods and services). This component may be reduced by the amount of redundancy and resilience supplied by other responding elements.

- **Economic** – encompasses the direct and indirect economic losses which include the cost to rebuild the asset, cost to respond to and recover from the attack, downstream costs resulting from the disruption of a product or service, and long-term costs due to environmental damage. The economic consequence component for ESSAT may be measured by the direct cost to completely replace a facility, responding capability assets, or the cost incurred in training, re-supply, or recovery of a capability element. Typically, this component is expressed in dollars and can assist in the risk management process when deciding which mitigation efforts to implement and the prioritizing of critical elements.

- **Psychological** – is the effect on public morale and confidence in national economic and political institutions, which encompasses those changes in perceptions emerging after a significant incident that affects the public's sense of safety and well-being and can manifest in aberrant behavior. This may be represented in the amount of increased response requests presented during an event and its subsequent effects due to an increased response time. A confidence scale of an affected population could also be used, which measures the confidence of emergency responders' ability to conduct their mission. These consequences would be very difficult to measure with any degree of certainty.

- **Governance/Mission Impact** – is the effect on government or industry's ability to maintain order, deliver minimum essential public services, ensure public health and safety, and carry out national security-related missions. All aspects of the Nation's critical infrastructure depend on a functioning Emergency Services Sector, which essentially means ensuring emergency responders are healthy and safe in the conduct of their roles. The mission component for ESSAT may relate to the amount of loss of services or core processes. This can be measured in an increased response time or in the decreased abilities of surrounding capability elements to respond, due to an increase in the amount of response incidents resulting from the incapacitation or loss of another element. Consequences in the ESS will have some degree of cascading effects to other CIKR.

3.4 Assessing Vulnerabilities

The base element for the vulnerability component is the ECIP security survey, which resides in the IST and utilizes the approved DHS IP vulnerability methodology. ECIP is currently capable of assessing fixed assets only, but will be expanded to incorporate systems analysis. The ECIP uses quantitative scoring indices for both vulnerability and protective measures, and is scored based on the absence of physical security measures and presence of protective measures, resulting in an overall protective measures index for the asset.

The main components of ECIP are physical security, security management, security forces, information sharing, protective measures, and dependencies. Each main component has subcomponents, which each have several more detailed characteristic components. Figure 3-3 shows a visual representation of the IST.

Figure 3-3: Infrastructure Survey Tool (IST)

Table 3-1: Physical Security, Security Management, and Security Force Subcomponents

Physical Security subcomponents	Security Management subcomponents	Security Force subcomponents
	Business continuity plans	Staffing
Fences	Security plans	Equipment
Gates	Emergency action plans	Weapons
Closed circuit television system	Threat levels	Training
Intrusion detection system	Security information communications	Post guidelines
Parking and access control	External security exercises	Patrols
Security lighting	Executive protection programs	Random patrols
Vehicle access control	Security working groups	After-hours security
Building envelope	Sensitive information identification	Command and control procedures
	National security clearances and background checks	Memorandums of understanding and memorandums of agreement

Table 3-2: Information Sharing, Protective Measures and Dependencies Subcomponents

Information Sharing subcomponents	Protective Measures subcomponents	Dependencies subcomponents
		Dependency on critical products
Threat sources	New protective measures	Electricity
Information sharing and mechanisms of information sharing	Random security measures	Information technology
Capturing these attributes will assist in determining the vulnerability level of susceptibility of loss of information sharing.	This component captures each full- or part-time measure that is employed and will contribute to the analysis of determining the likelihood of a successful attack.	Natural gas
		Telecommunications
		Transportation, water, and wastewater
		Through a cross-sector working group, dependencies can be fully realized.

3.5 Assessing Threats

The final component in the risk equation is threat. Generally, when calculating risk, the threat of an intentional hazard is estimated as the likelihood of an attack that accounts for both the intent and capability of the adversary; for other hazards, threat is generally estimated as the likelihood that a hazard will occur.

The ESSAT will incorporate pre-established threat profiles for critical assets that are unique to each individual threat or asset scenario. The threat profile will be determined by considering the characteristics of each applicable threat, the individual asset, and the likelihood or rate of occurrence for that threat. For example, when considering the threat of a hurricane, a 9-1-1 Call Center located in Florida will have a higher rate of occurrence than a similar facility located in Ohio.

The final ESS risk methodology will consider the full spectrum of intentional and unintentional threats including:

- Natural threats (e.g., hurricane, fire, and floods);

- Manmade threats (e.g., chemical, radiological, and biological attacks);

- Workforce threats (e.g., pandemic flu, insider threat, and human error); and

- Cyber-related threats (e.g., technological hazard and degradation of CAD system).

In addition to contagious human diseases and cyber attacks, complex, coordinated attacks with multiple events affecting a large geographical region or multiple regions pose a significant threat to the sector. An attack of this magnitude would impact severely the sector's resilience and sustainability. Although the sector is robust and has built-in redundant systems, multiple or widely distributed attacks could exhaust State, regional, and local resources.

In the assessment of terrorist threats, ESS will consider both capability and intent as discrete subcomponents of threat. The NIPP defines threat capability as the availability or the ease of use of tools or methods that could potentially be used to damage, disrupt, or destroy critical functions. The sector will continuously draw on both national and local intelligence sources so that sector partners will better understand the threat intent and capability on a near real-time basis. An example of a national source for threat information and analysis includes the DHS HITRAC, which facilitates the annual SHIRA process.

Unlike manmade threats, natural hazards are more predictable based on the availability of historical natural hazards data. ESS will analyze these types of potential threats and determine those of national and regional significance for application in the threat portion of the sector risk assessment. Threat assessments are generally applicable to a geographic region or threat source. Figure 3-4 is a visual representation of different sources of threat.

Figure 3-4: Threat Sources

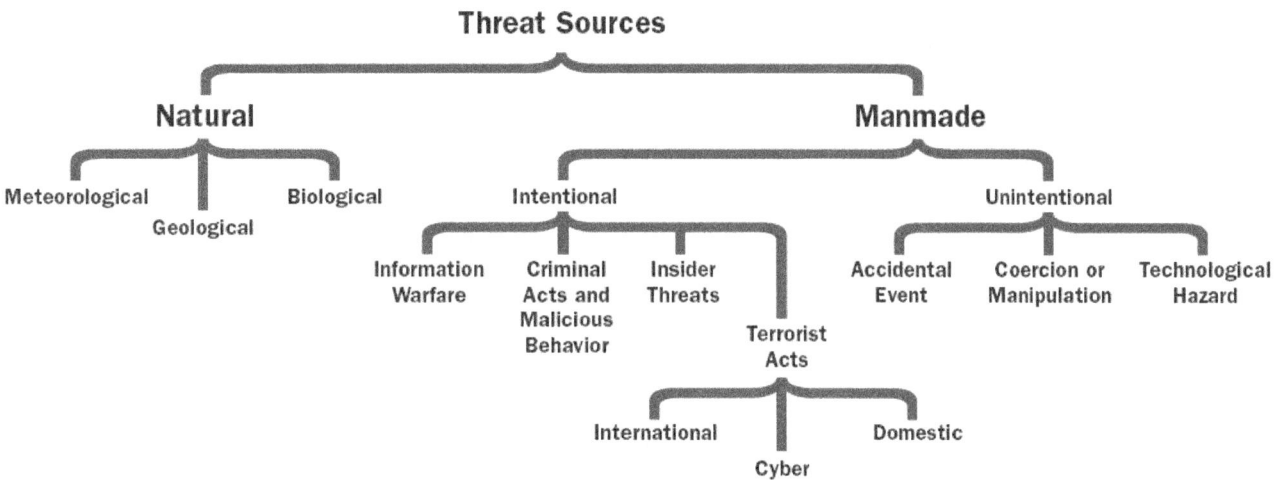

3.6 Success Factors

The implementation of the ESS risk assessment approach requires commitment from all sector partners. The ES SSA, GCC, and SCC acknowledge that sharing and updating information and assessments of threats, vulnerabilities, consequences, and protective programs are essential to developing a valid ESS risk assessment. A collaborative working group of sector partners will implement the national and regional ESS risk assessment approach. The success of the ESS risk management process is dependent on participation and support from all sector stakeholders.

As risks are assessed across the sector, it is important to note that risk is not static. Threats, vulnerabilities, and consequences are dynamic, and changes can come from a variety of sources. Thus, it is vital that baseline information and assessments are updated regularly to reflect the changing environment and its impact on risk.

4. Prioritize Infrastructure

The ESS infrastructure and associated protective programs must be prioritized based on risk to ensure that the sector applies resources in areas that will most enhance the mitigation of risk. The sector cannot protect every element of its infrastructure against all possible threats. Affordability, return on investment, and sustainability are key considerations in determining which shortfalls will be addressed immediately or over time. Systematic methods for prioritizing sector assets, as well as any corresponding protective actions, offer direction and increase the defensibility of resource allocation decisions. This chapter focuses on risk-based processes that are still in development and are designed to facilitate the prioritization of assets within ESS.

Figure 4-1: Prioritize Infrastructure

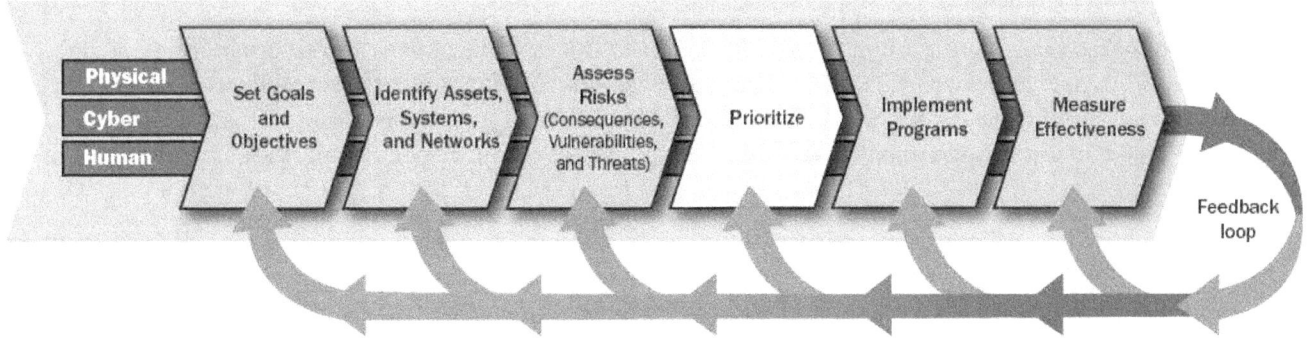

Continuous improvement to enhance protection of CIKR

As described in chapter 3, there are three general risk assessment layers: (1) facility-specific or fixed assets, (2) specialized emergency services assets or systems, and (3) multiple systems in a region or multiple regions. As with risk assessment in general, each risk assessment layer has individual aspects of prioritization, yet builds on the other layers, rolling up multiple systems into a regional perspective. Facility risk priorities generally relate to an individual facility (e.g., fire or police stations, 9-1-1 call centers, or emergency operations centers). System risk priorities generally relate to the elements that build the system and the entities that rely on and manage the 9-1-1 call centers, HAZMAT, or SWAT teams. Regional risk priorities relate to multiple systems and multiple echelons of concern.

Generally, the respective facility manager, emergency service leader, or emergency manager will prioritize the facility-specific or fixed asset risk mitigation. The ESSAT, as it matures, is expected to give the facility a comparison of like facilities, including a comparison across the risk management perspective (e.g., physical security, contingency planning, and dependencies).

Individual system directors or managers (e.g., individual HAZMAT or SWAT team leadership), or regional emergency managers or planners are expected to execute the system asset risk mitigation prioritization. The sector expects the ESSAT will give a comparison of like systems. This would include aspects such as the security and training of specialized equipment and personnel, levels or limits of response capabilities, areas of distribution, and areas of response coverage.

The ESSAT is envisioned to contain general threat comparisons, cross-sector comparisons, threat-specific comparisons, and an overall vulnerability calculation. This will provide direction to regional emergency managers or planners and emergency service leadership, and increase the defensibility of resource allocation decisions.

DHS stresses all-hazards preparedness that requires attention to a wide range of events and regional geographic and demographic perspectives in relation to risk gaps. The mitigation of risk gaps drives sector resource requirements. Each factor (threat, vulnerability, or consequence) of the risk equation and the relative importance of existing risk gaps are also considered when determining prioritization of protective initiatives. The factor driving an asset's risk profile can be used to plan appropriate protective measures (e.g., a plan that focuses on reducing vulnerabilities versus consequences), thus allowing the prioritization process to serve not only as a resource allocation process, but also as a way to help design, facilitate, and implement protective programs. This simple risk assessment framework provides the ability to consider tradeoffs between objectives and constraints when determining the priority protective programs.

There is a fine line between DHS agencies when considering the ESS response perspective and the ESS infrastructure protection perspective that affects the prioritization of risk functions for the sector. FEMA is the Federal lead for response, and IP is the Federal lead for the protection of ESS assets, systems, and networks. It is important to note that the CIKR priorities for the sector cannot be determined in isolation of the response priorities; therefore, FEMA and IP must work in close collaboration to lead a coordinated national effort to mitigate risk.

When considering the protection and risk mitigation efforts from a CIKR view, the sector is focused inwardly at protecting the sector assets, systems, and networks. This inward view ultimately affects the response mission of the sector, as without protection measures in place the sector cannot fill that mission. The loss of ESS assets, systems, and networks ultimately results in a negative impact to the civilian community either from delayed response or no response to an attack, natural disaster, or other emergency.

ESS operates in a dynamic environment wherein threats, vulnerabilities, and consequences can vary over time. This necessitates a continuous cycle of risk and capability assessment updates to ensure that operational decisions are grounded in superior situational awareness. As the risk changes, prioritization and protection should change accordingly.

5. Develop and Implement Protective Programs and Resilience Strategies

The mission of the ESS is to save lives, protect property and the environment, assist communities impacted by disasters and aid recovery from emergency situations. The sector's unique dual mission of protecting the public as well as the sector itself places it in a unique position as both the "protector" and the "protected." The CIKR partnership vision is an ESS in which facilities, key support systems, information and coordination systems, and personnel are protected from both ordinary operational risks and from extraordinary risks or attacks. The dual protection mission of the sector—prevent, protect against, respond to, and recover from an incident—is indistinguishable from the CIKR mission, which is the same, albeit directed at the sector itself.

Figure 5-1: Develop and Implement Protective Programs and Resilience Strategies

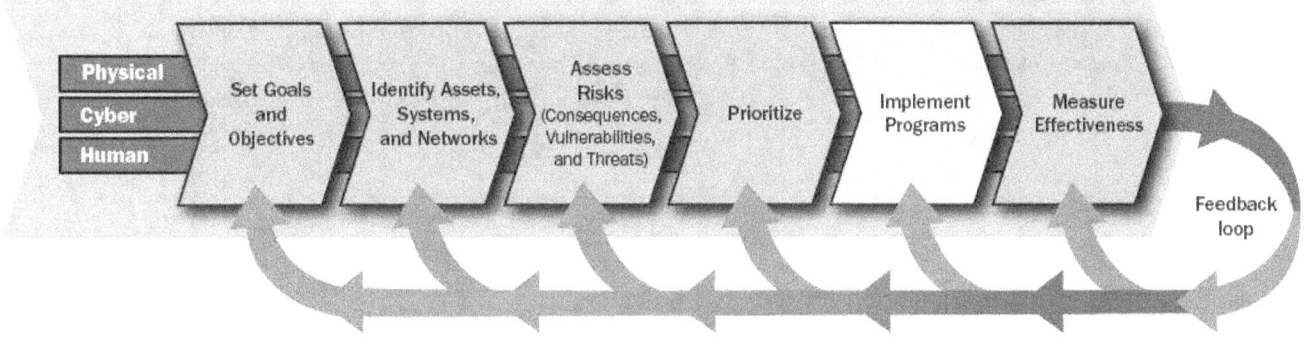

Continuous Improvement to enhance protection of CIKR

5.1. Overview of Sector Protective Programs and Resilience Strategies

Due to the all-encompassing nature of ES missions, the sector's protective programs and resilience strategies focus on preparedness, which crosses the entire Protective Spectrum of prevention, protection, response, and recovery from an incident, as shown in Figure 5-2 below. Enhanced preparedness translates to a more secure and resilient ESS. Numerous protective programs exist throughout the sector that involve measures designed to prevent, deter, and mitigate threats; reduce vulnerability to attack or other disasters; minimize consequences; and enable timely, efficient response and restoration following events and natural or manmade disasters, including cyber attacks. It is important to note: these protective programs that contribute to the protection and resilience of the sector are very diverse, and are developed by numerous Federal, State, local, tribal, and territorial agencies, trade associations representing each of the disciplines, and education and training institutions that support the sector's specialized capabilities.

Figure 5-2: The Protective Spectrum

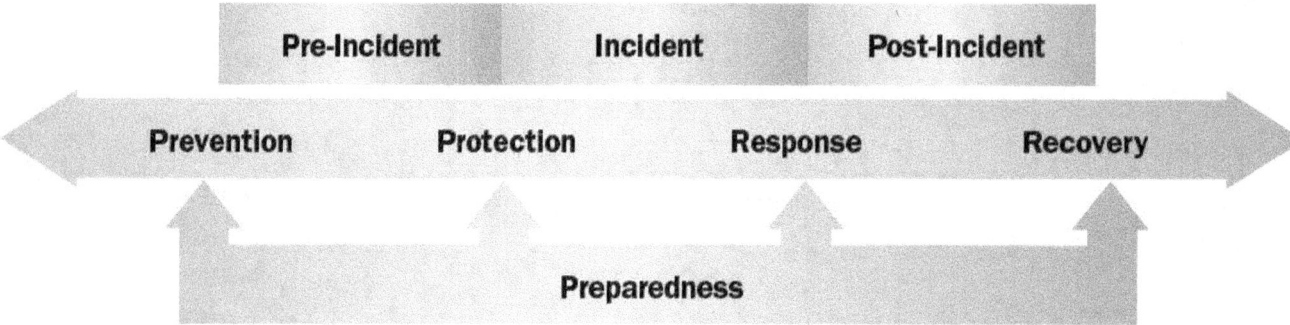

Emergency responders view risk from an all-hazards perspective, and thus, any type of incident, whether manmade or natural, poses potential risk to the responder. Effective ESS protective programs and resilience strategies mitigate consequences, vulnerabilities, and threats to the sector, and are tailored to meet its diversity. The sector's approach to defining and analyzing risk involves three separate paths:

• Risk associated with fixed facilities, such as EOCs and PSAPs;

• Risk to specialized capabilities; and

• Risk to ESS assets, systems, and networks in an affected region or area.

ESS protective programs are influenced by the risk management process, national preparedness priorities, and regional assessments, such as DHS Protective Security Coordination Division's Regional Resiliency Assessment Program, Buffer Zone Protection Program, and Site Assistance Visits. Additionally, there are a wide variety of activities conducted at the State and local levels that drive ESS protective programs and resilience strategies, such as the ongoing FEMA regional gap analysis that originated at the national level following lessons learned after hurricane Katrina.

5.1.1 Cybersecurity Programs

The nature of the ESS makes broad generalization of cyber systems usage difficult. Although some similarities exist, each discipline uses cyber systems differently in its daily activities. A lack of standards, combined with variations in organization, diversity of assets, availability of resources, and other factors combine to create a very diverse and dynamic cyber landscape. To enhance the cybersecurity posture of the sector, the ESS CSWG, a subcomponent of the ESS Information Sharing Working Group (ISWG), is charged with developing a comprehensive strategy for the sector. At a minimum, the strategy will promote an awareness of cybersecurity issues, identify cyber threats and vulnerabilities, prioritize and recommend protective programs and resilience strategies, and facilitate implementation of protective methodologies to help State and local governments with protective metrics, compliance inventory and assessment, and audit of protective assets.

As identified in chapter 1, many ESS activities are conducted in cyberspace, such as EOCs, database management, biometric activities, telecommunications, and electronic systems (i.e., security systems) are vulnerable to cyber attack. Additionally, the Internet is widely used by the sector to provide information and receive alerts, warnings, and threats relevant to the ESS.

Within DHS, NCSD provides robust cyber programs committed to proactively developing preparedness measures through increased awareness and information sharing. NCSD is DHS' lead agency for securing cyberspace and our Nation's cyber assets, and is recognized as a leading advocate for cybersecurity investments and activities. A comprehensive, but not exclusive listing and description of the existing cyber programs is included in Appendix 4.

ES partners may receive cyber alerts through US-CERT, which is the Federal Government's principal cyber watch and warning center responsible for analyzing and reducing cyber threats and vulnerabilities, disseminating cyber threat warning information, and coordinating incident response activities. The MS-ISAC is another program that electronically sends cyber alerts to the sector and is discussed in detail in chapter 1. Additionally, the ES SSA participates in DHS' CSCSWG, which identifies opportunities to improve sector coordination around cybersecurity issues and topics, highlights cyber dependencies and interdependencies, and shares government and private sector cybersecurity products and findings. The SSA provides relevant feedback to the SCC regarding cybersecurity initiatives that arise from the CSCSWG and impact the sector.

5.1.2 Sector Partner Collaboration and Coordination

Many ESS protective programs and initiatives that exist at the Federal, State, and local levels, as well as within the private sector, go unnoticed or unrecognized at the national or congressional level. It is the goal of the ES SSA to promote these collaborative efforts among all sector partners dedicated to the protection of the sector. Such collaboration contributes to the development of robust plans, protocols, and processes that represent a regional and national interest.

The ES SSA uses a Sector Initiatives Call (SIC) to collate and catalogue the multitude of protective activities related to ESS CIKR projects. The data call was first initiated with the ESS GCC, and the ES SSA is working with the ES SCC to obtain similar data. The data call occurs a minimum of twice a year, and coincides with the GCC and SCC joint meetings. As a result of the data calls, the ES SSA develops and maintains a comprehensive database of programs. Additionally, the intent is to post the data on the HSIN-CS/ESS portal to provide visibility to all sector partners.

In general, ongoing collaboration exists among the ESS partners to identify, develop, and coordinate protective programs and resilience strategies and initiatives. At a minimum, communication occurs through Web-based portals, regularly scheduled GCC and SCC meetings, e-mails, and participation in sector working groups.

5.2 Determining Protective Program Needs and Resilience Strategies

The complexities and vastness of the sector make it difficult to capture its enormous programmatic needs. Given the size and diversity of the ESS, there is no one-size-fits-all protective solution. Each of the sector disciplines determines its individual needs as well as the sector's collective program needs through a variety of mechanisms. The process for determining the need for protective programs or resilience strategies transcends the entire protective spectrum (prevention, protection, response, and recovery). One method is for the sector to organize around the National Preparedness Guidelines, which identify high priority gaps at the national level, and, in turn, inform the types of eligible protective programs for grant funding. Additionally, gaps are identified through exercise participation and evaluation, current and emerging threat patterns, and risk assessment activities. Partnership engagement with the GCC and SCC is critical to understanding the CIKR gaps within the sector, as well as being informed through the work of councils such as the Interagency Board (IAB) and the National Homeland Security Council. Conferences also provide a forum for discussions about common gaps in prevention, preparedness, and protection activities. These opportunities for dialogue provide mechanisms to identify program needs for the sector. The SSA and SCC work collaboratively to consolidate and communicate the common protective program priorities of the sector from a national perspective.

5.2.1 Identifying Gaps and Determining Program Needs

The National Preparedness Guidelines establish a vision for preparedness and a systematic methodology for assessing needs and prioritizing preparedness efforts across the Nation. The Target Capabilities List (included in the National Preparedness Guidelines), describes the collective national capabilities required to prevent, protect against, respond to, and recover from terrorist attacks, major disasters, and other emergencies. Using the National Preparedness Guidelines as a compass, each year DHS awards billions of dollars in grants to States, urban areas, and transportation authorities through 14 programs to bolster national preparedness capabilities and protect critical infrastructure. One of the largest grant programs within DHS is the

Homeland Security Grant Program, which totals more than $1.7 billion. Other multiple infrastructure protection programs total more than $845 million. Each year, grant funding focuses on specific priorities that are tailored to either States or urban areas. In turn, these priorities influence the sector priorities. Examples of national priorities considered by the sector as needing strengthening include the following:

- Preparedness planning, training and exercises;

- Improvised explosive devices (IEDs) and IED deterrence, prevention, protection, and response capabilities;

- Information-sharing capabilities and communication interoperability;

- Medical readiness through enhanced medical surge capability and mass prophylaxis;

- Preventive radiological/nuclear detection capabilities; and

- CBRNE capabilities.

In addition, the Interoperable Emergency Communications Grant Program (IECGP) is a grant program created in response to the September 11th attacks. The IECGP is being administered as a joint effort between DHS Office of Emergency Communications (OEC) and the Federal Emergency Management Agency (FEMA) Grant Programs Directorate (GPD). In both Fiscal Year 2008 (FY 2008) and FY 2009, about $50 million was made available for IECGP grants to States and Territories. The State Administrative Agencies of the 56 States and Territories are the eligible applicants for this grant program. All activities proposed under IECGP must be integral to interoperable emergency communications, and must align with the goals, objectives, and initiatives identified in the grantee's approved Statewide Communications Interoperability Plan and the National Emergency Communications Plan. Funding for the first two years of the program focused on Leadership and Governance, Common Planning and Operational Protocols, and Emergency Responder Skills and Capabilities.

Other targeted grant programs that influence the sector's approach to identifying needs include fire grants, focused on the safety and training of firefighters; emergency management grants, which enhance the skills of emergency managers; and acquisition and training grants, which support the acquisition of and training for new technology or equipment.

Gaps in prevention, preparedness, response, and recovery program needs may be identified during responses to real incidents, or through exercises that practice and refine responses to a variety of potential disruptions. Numerous government and private sector exercises are carried out almost daily. The evaluation of performance during these exercises is important to determine if responders have the capacity to respond effectively to an incident and to identify vulnerability gaps where improvement is necessary. Exercises provide the sector insight as to the capabilities and deficiencies requiring further attention. Not all deficiencies lead to a specific program need, but they do contribute to the overall assessment of program needs for the sector. Additionally, the DHS-funded nonprofit National Memorial Institute for the Prevention of Terrorism established the Lessons Learned Information Sharing Web site (**www.llis.gov**), which gives registered users access to substantial preparedness information, including after action reports on various exercises. This information provides the sector with an opportunity to compare itself against others and to identify common capability gap trends across the Nation.

The sector's risk assessment program is another mechanism to identify gaps and assists with the prioritization of protective programs. The selection of protective programs based on risk ensures that resources are applied in areas that will most enhance risk mitigation. In addition to assessment of risk, the sector also takes into account the current and emerging threat environment, then factors in the potential consequences of not initiating a protective measure for an identified gap. Threat information may cause the sector to develop protective measures to mitigate that threat.

To provide sector awareness of cybersecurity gaps, the sector is collaborating with NCSD in the use of the Cybersecurity Evaluation Tool (CSET). The CSET is a DHS product that assists organizations in protecting key cyber assets. This tool provides the sector an approach for assessing the cybersecurity posture of its information systems and networks. Site Assistance Visits, combined with the use of the CSET, allow the sector to prioritize risk mitigation activities and identify protective programs that assist in enhancing the cybersecurity resilience of the sector.

Many ESS issues, programs, and initiatives are being addressed through numerous Federal programs (i.e., FEMA, USFA, S&T, IICD, NCSD, Intelligence and Analysis (I&A), OBP, SLTTGCC). The sector remains vigilant in its efforts to capture and focus the activities pertaining to ESS CIKR to reduce duplication of efforts. Similarly, a significant amount of activity focused on ESS is conducted internally within the disciplines in which the SCC associations have visibility and are in a position to provide guidance and direction to the sector. As a result, it is imperative that the ES SSA, GCC, and SCC work closely together to optimally impact the security and resilience of the sector CIKR. Members of the SCC, GCC, and SSA update one another regarding sector activities through frequent e-mails, meetings, conference attendance, and teleconferences.

5.2.2 Determining Protective Program and Resilience Strategy Priorities

The sector cannot protect every element of its infrastructure against all possible threats. Affordability, return on investment, and sustainability are key considerations in determining which gaps will be addressed immediately or over time. Systematic methods for prioritizing sector assets, as well as any corresponding protective actions, offer direction and increase the defensibility of resource allocation decisions.

As discussed in chapter 4, each risk assessment layer has individual aspects of prioritization, yet builds on the other layers, rolling up multiple systems to ascertain a regional perspective. The layers of risk priorities include facilities, systems/networks, and regional aspects which entail multiple systems and multiple echelons of concern. Additionally, each factor (threat, vulnerability, or consequence) of the risk equation and the relative importance of existing risk gaps are considered when determining prioritization of protective initiatives.

Risk mitigation activities (RMAs) or protective measures are essential to diminishing the risks and vulnerabilities of the sector. Several factors influence the prioritization of these programs as sector partners in each discipline have distinct assets, operational processes, and risk management approaches. RMAs are voluntary and developed by many governmental agencies, from the Federal to the local level, in an effort to improve the sector's protective posture. RMAs protect the ESS assets, systems, and networks, and are generally prioritized around information sharing, interoperable communications, and response capability improvement. The effective coordination of the prioritization and implementation of activities that impact emergency responders continues to be a challenge among all Federal agencies and within IP.

It is crucial that the SSA, in collaboration with the GCC and SCC, proceed ahead with a clear understanding of the most effective strategies to avoid common pitfalls and to capitalize on measures that share best practices and economies of scale whenever possible.

The SSA and SCC are fully engaged in developing strategies to communicate existing protective programs, lessons learned, and best practices to the sector to enable effective prioritization of efforts. As discussed earlier, the SSA initiated a Sector Initiatives Call with the GCC to capture numerous activities impacting the ESS, which are communicated to the sector at regularly scheduled SCC and GCC meetings. Furthermore, associations involved with ES SCC are developing measures to communicate to their constituents. For example, the International Association of Fire Chiefs (IAFC) formed an Economic Challenge Task Force which posts the task force resources on its Web site. The IAFC goals are to understand the "most effective strategies" and to share "best practices;" this effort includes consolidating recommendations from all emergency responders.

As discussed, there are numerous avenues the sector uses to identify gaps leading to the development of protective programs. Ultimately, the SSA works with all sector partners to develop processes and strategies to identify and validate protective program needs and actions, and evaluate existing programs that could be used to fill those gaps. The basic premise used when evaluating existing programs is guided by the characteristics of effective CIKR programs and resilience strategies laid out in the NIPP. These characteristics include:

- Comprehensive: Effective programs must address the physical, cyber, and human elements of CIKR, as appropriate, and must consider long-term, short-term, and sustainable activities;

- Coordinated: Effective programs must coordinate with others. Because of the highly complex nature of the ESS, efficient coordination of protective programs to avoid duplication of effort is an enormous challenge, and probably the most prevalent within the sector;

- Cost-effective: Effective CIKR strategies and programs should focus on actions that offer the greatest mitigation of risk for any given expenditure; and

- Risk-informed: Protective programs and resilience strategies should focus on mitigating risk. Measurement, evaluation, and feedback provide information on the success of the ability to "buy down risk."

5.3 Protective Program Implementation

Implementation of protective measures involves commitment of resources in the form of people, equipment, materials, time, and money. ESS assets, systems, and networks are widely diverse and geographically distributed, requiring both sector partner and national leadership involvement to ensure implementation of a comprehensive, coordinated, and cost-effective approach that helps reduce or manage risks to the Nation.

Numerous protective measures and strategies are developed and implemented at all levels of government and the private sector within the ESS. The ES SSA strives to coordinate those programs that impact risk to the Nation by narrowing its focus to the national, regional, or State level, as opposed to focusing on programs at the local level where the sector partner assumes more of an individual role in implementing protective measures specific to the location. For these large-scale programs, the SSA collaborates with the GCC and SCC, often through CIPAC working groups, in all phases of program implementation. A crucial step prior to implementation is to conduct a pilot program which is developed in collaboration with the GCC and SCC. This allows an opportunity for the sector to refine its program prior to implementation.

As stated previously, the SSA collaborates extensively with numerous Federal agencies that develop programs impacting the sector. As many ESS protective programs and initiatives are implemented through one or more Federal agencies, both external and internal to DHS, the SSA assumes more of an organizing role to avoid redundancy, confusion, and frustration on the part of the sector.

Additionally, to assist the sector in the coordination of cross-sector programs that impact ESS, the SSA is a major stakeholder in infrastructure protection-related councils or working groups, such as SLTTGCC, the CSCSWG, and others, that involve any of the 18 CIKR sectors. Another mechanism for cross-sector communication is through the Sector-Specific Agency Executive Management Office (SSA EMO), of which the ESS is one of six sectors. The sectors within SSA EMO conduct weekly meetings that provide a forum for discussions related to sector-specific programs and an opportunity to identify cross-sector implications. Once cross-sector programs are identified, the SSAs and sector partners work together to facilitate implementation.

5.4 Monitoring Program Implementation

Monitoring program implementation through accomplishment of milestones provides one indication as to the accomplishments of a program and whether results are being achieved. The sector receives information on how resources and efforts are allocated to ensure effectiveness and keeps sector partners focused on the key goals of a program. Additionally established milestones support development and justification of budget proposals through cost-benefit analysis.

ESS programs often have a deterrence, prevention, or preparedness focus, which can be difficult to monitor and measure for a variety of reasons. For example, it is difficult to measure accurately a program or activity that has deterrence as one of its primary goals. The absence of an attack or other negative event does not demonstrate the success of the program or activity, and the known or unknown factors that may have had an impact cannot be measured. Therefore, it is difficult to quantify whether the cost of a deterrence program or activity is justified. Modeling is one process used to determine effective protective programs or resilience strategies that merit continued support. Modeling can determine how well the deterrence process is functioning and demonstrate how the milestones are tied to the eventual outcome.

Data are needed to quantify the progress of the development and implementation of any program or resilience strategy, and measure its effectiveness. Monitoring the implementation of protective programs includes ensuring that collection of data is accurate, cost-effective, and efficient. The SSA works collaboratively with all sector partners to identify the most efficient and cost-effective process to collect the data to avoid multiple data calls for the same information. The ES SSA works extensively with IICD to stay attuned to the most comprehensive technological developments that may improve or modify the current methods for collecting and consolidating data.

Active involvement by the SSA and sector partners in R&D activities at the private sector, collegiate, Federal, State and local levels helps ensure that the sector is kept abreast of technological developments that may improve or modify protective programs and resilience strategies. As noted in chapter 7, sector subject matter experts participate in guiding the R&D projects conducted through S&T and the SSA is kept informed through participation in various meetings. The IAB, which is comprised of practitioners, is yet another mechanism to recommend R&D activities for the sector and involves sector partner subject matter expert participation. As mentioned previously, the sector remains informed of R&D activities through annual reports, discussion at meetings, and Web sites.

This SSP has documented many avenues for communicating best practices and lessons learned to the sector. A great many of the mechanisms used to share information are Web-based and include Federal sites such as the EMR-ISAC, the HSIN-CS/ESS Portal, the Responder Knowledge Base Portal, and Lessons Learned Information Sharing Web site. Additionally, association Web sites customarily include a section devoted to best practices and lessons learned that communicate effectiveness of protective programs and resilience strategies. Other methods the sector routinely uses to share information include presenting at conferences and publishing white papers, story boards, and poster presentations. Partners may want to consider these and other methods when determining the most effective strategies for their locality. Lastly, the GCC and SCC conduct regularly scheduled meetings and conference calls where protective programs are sometimes discussed and dialogue ensues relative to protective strategies affecting a specific discipline or the sector as a whole.

6. Measure Effectiveness

Measuring effectiveness is the final chevron in the NIPP risk management framework, and establishes the mechanism by which CIKR protection activities are improved. The NIPP requires a metrics-based system of performance evaluation to establish accountability, document performance, facilitate diagnoses, and promote effective management. Metrics supply the data needed to measure progress toward specific goals and to show what corrective actions may be beneficial. Measurement is a shared responsibility between DHS and its CIKR partners, including Federal, State, local, tribal, territorial, and private sector stakeholders.

Figure 6-1: NIPP Risk Management Framework: Measure Effectiveness

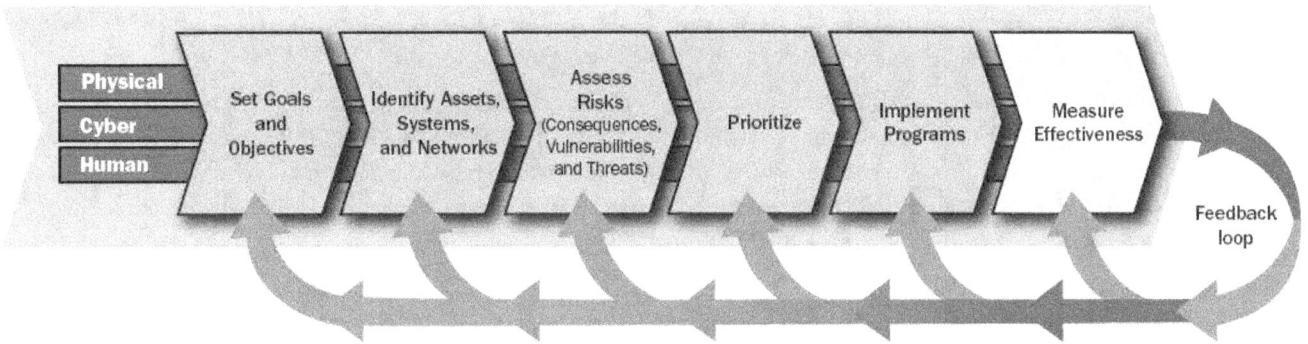

6.1 Risk Mitigation Activities

The ESS meets NIPP metrics program requirements by identifying key RMAs and developing metrics to measure their progress. This section of the SSP describes the processes the sector uses to develop the RMAs and identify those that are most vital to the sector.

An RMA, as defined by the NIPP Measurement and Reporting Office, is "a program, tool, initiative, project, major task, or some other undertaking that directly or indirectly leads to a reduction in risk."

ESS RMAs are essential to diminishing the risks and vulnerabilities of the sector. Factors that influence the development of each RMA include the distinct assets, operational processes, and risk management approaches of each sector discipline. The RMA initiatives involve measures designed to:

- Prevent, deter, and mitigate threats;
- Reduce vulnerability to attack or other disasters;
- Minimize consequences; and
- Enable timely, efficient response and restoration following events and natural or manmade disasters, including cyber attack.

The ESS conducts an annual review of its RMAs to identify and prioritize the activities that will have the greatest impact on risk mitigation for the sector.

6.2 Process for Measuring Effectiveness

NIPP metrics are reported in two ways: National Coordinator Progress Indicators and Sector Progress Indicators. National Coordinator Progress Indicators describe DHS IP efforts to support NIPP and SSP-related activities. Sector Progress Indicators collectively describe the progress made by each sector and the effectiveness of activities within the CIKR sectors.

The National Coordinator Progress Indicators are reported in the National CIKR Protection Annual Report (National Annual Report). Metrics discussed in this document are considered ES Sector Progress Indicators. The types of data collected to assess the progress of RMAs include:

- **Descriptive Data** provide RMA progress or explain the beneficial value of RMAs achieved during the reporting period. Examples include the number of ESS systems, or the percentage of ESS facilities owned by the private sector;

- **Output Data** gauge whether specific activities were performed as planned, track the progression of a task, or report on the output of a process. Output data show progress in performing the activities necessary to achieve CIKR protection goals and can serve as leading indicators for outcome measures. They also help build a comprehensive picture of the sector's CIKR protection status and activities. Examples include the number and frequency of security patrols at an ESS facility or the number of ESS owners who performed vulnerability assessments in the previous year; and

- **Outcome Data** indicate progress, value, or beneficial results toward achieving a strategic goal and associated target rather than level of activity. A high-level metric may demonstrate national achievement of risk mitigation as a result of implementation of a particular CIKR protection initiative. Examples include the change in number of ESS systems assessed as high risk following the implementation of protective actions.

6.2.1 Process for Measuring Sector Progress

The development of outcome metrics can be a challenging process because it requires taking intangible concepts (e.g., risk mitigation, implementation of the sector partnership model) and putting boundaries around the concept in order to measure progress, value, or beneficial results toward achieving a strategic goal. Developing an outcome-based measurement program takes time, and data are not immediately available. The ESS also faces challenges in developing outcome metrics when there are multiple activities or uncontrollable factors impacting a desired outcome. For example, the ESS relies on voluntary distribution channels and currently has no mechanism to track the information pathway. Despite these challenges, the ESS is committed to measuring program effectiveness and progress in implementing the NIPP risk management framework.

Currently, the ES SSA has assembled a list of RMAs for the sector. The SSA developed this list by soliciting GCC and SCC representatives for activities, programs, tools, and initiatives that lead to risk reduction for the sector. The SSA staff analyzes the assembled list of RMAs to first identify those that are most vital to the sector. These key activities are assessed for possible avenues of measuring progress and effectiveness.

As the process matures, sector participation is expected to increase and expand. The nomination of sector members will continue and increased member involvement is necessary in determining key activities and measuring effectiveness and progress.

6.2.2 Information Collection and Verification

The SSA is responsible for collecting the data needed to measure and quantify progress in development and implementation of the risk management framework for the sector. The SSA works collaboratively with all sector partners to identify the most efficient and cost-effective process for collecting the data annually, unless stated otherwise. Currently, the sector is working to overcome the many challenges it faces, including:

- Lack of a single source or repository for data collection;
- Complexity and variety of organizations that compose a sector;
- Costs of surveys;
- Low response rates to surveys; and
- Concern in sharing sensitive information on assets and security measures.

The ESS coordinates with existing working groups and multiagency partnerships that include subject matter experts; owners and operators; and Federal, State, local, tribal, territorial, and private stakeholders to develop metrics data on the sector's risk mitigation activities. Subsequent outreach to stakeholders updates and verifies the data collected. Information gleaned through outreach activities strengthens and supports sector protective programs.

6.2.3 Reporting

As required by HSPD-7, the SSA provides its Sector CIKR Protection Annual Report (Sector Annual Report) to the Secretary of Homeland Security. The Sector Annual Report outlines the sector's progress on identifying, prioritizing, and coordinating protection of CIKR within the sector. In collaboration with the SSA, GCC, and SCC, DHS determines the evaluative criteria and the format used for measuring progress. The SSA then collates the results, which the GCC and SCC validate prior to publication and distribution throughout the sector. The SSA, in collaboration with the GCC and SCC, uses the evaluative data to track the accomplishment of sector goals and provide the rationale for goal or program revision.

6.3 Using Metrics for Continuous Improvement

Metrics data provide a mechanism to compare the sector's performance with its goals. The SSA and its sector partners can adjust the sector's CIKR protection approach to account for progress achieved, identify areas of improvement, and recognize opportunities to develop the sector goals and objectives further. To some extent, as protective programs are implemented the consequences and vulnerabilities associated with the assets may be mitigated.

Accordingly, the sector coordinates with HITRAC to develop the current and emerging national threat perspective, which is used in determining a national risk profile. In addition to an increased understanding of potential system-wide cascading consequences, the national risk profile can influence current and prospective allocation of resources. In addition to supporting the evaluation of program progress against sector priorities, metrics serve as a feedback mechanism for other parts of the NIPP risk management framework and note its progress toward sector goals. This approach promotes continuous improvement by using the data garnered from data collection and measurement efforts to inform protective program implementation and development.

7. CIKR Protection Research and Development

Research and development (R&D) plays a significant role in enabling homeland security partners to develop knowledge and technologies that more effectively reduce risk to the Nation's CIKR. The ESS is made up of very diverse disciplines and supporting elements with missions that address a wide variety of terrorist and natural threats to the homeland. New and innovative technology-based solutions are required to prevent or mitigate the potential effects of current and future dangers, including the numerous challenges faced by the disciplines and supporting elements that are integral to providing protection for the sector. Generally, the CIKR R&D focus for the sector is to influence R&D activities at the Federal level, furthering a comprehensive approach that encompasses both operational and CIKR R&D needs.

7.1 Overview of Sector Protective Programs and Resilience Strategies

Pursuant to HSPD-7, the White House Office of Science and Technology Policy (OSTP) is responsible for coordinating inter-agency R&D to enhance the protection of CIKR. OSTP, which was established in 1976, provides expert advice to the President in all areas of science and technology. HSPD-7 mandates a national plan that systematically harnesses the Nation's capabilities and provides the long-term technology advances needed for more effective and cost-efficient protection of CIKR. As directed by HSPD-7, the Secretary of Homeland Security shall work in coordination with the Director of OSTP to develop the annual Federal R&D Plan.

The Homeland Security Act of 2002 designated DHS S&T the responsibility of advising the Secretary on R&D requirements, priorities, and programs that support the DHS vision and mission. Additionally, S&T is responsible for developing and integrating technology to support the national CIKR protection strategies, policies, and procedures. As a result, DHS S&T plays a significant role in the R&D efforts of the ESS. DHS S&T works to understand, document and offer solutions to current and anticipated threats faced by first responders through Capstone Integrated Product Teams (IPT). The IPT process is a requirements-driven, output-oriented methodology that ensures quality and efficacious products are developed in close alignment with the first responder community. Capstone IPTs exist across the 13 major homeland security core functional areas: Information Sharing/ Management, Cybersecurity, People Screening, Border Security, Chemical/Biological Defense, Maritime Security, Counter-Improvised Explosive Devices, Infrastructure Protection, Transportation Security, Incident Management, Interoperability, Cargo Security and First Responder. As these IPTs support R&D requirements for the sector, the challenge for the ES SSA is to stay abreast of the numerous projects across multiple IPTs to ensure they meet the strategic needs of the sector.

Another prominent group representing first responders is the IAB, a user working group supported by voluntary participation from various Federal, State, and local government and private organizations. This working group provides Federal partners a prioritized, cross-cutting view of critical issues in technology and R&D related to the sector. A subgroup of the IAB, the Science Technology Committee identifies inter-agency (Federal, State, and local) first responder R&D requirements and innovative technologies that address all-hazards detection, individual and collective protection, medical support, decontamination, communications systems, information technology, training, and operational support.

FEMA administers the alert and warning system for DHS in partnership with DHS S&T, the Federal Communications Commission, National Oceanic and Atmospheric Administration (NOAA), the U.S. Department of Justice's Office of Justice Programs for AMBER Alerts, the Joint Interoperability Test Command, and other Federal partners. The Integrated Public Alert Warning System (IPAWS) Program Management Office is also engaged with the FEMA Regions in order to coordinate requirements of regional, State, and local emergency managers.

The American public is our greatest stakeholder. As with any disaster situation, it is the strength and resilience of the American people that ameliorates the initial devastating impact of a disaster, regardless of its origin. FEMA and the IPAWS Program Management Office will work to ensure, through the many forums and venues available, that the needs and concerns of the public are known and integrated into the next generation of alert and warning.

Coordinating R&D efforts is challenging for large, complex infrastructure sectors, such as the ESS, with numerous stakeholders, assets, and priorities. DHS IP recognizes this challenge and provides assistance to SCCs, GCCs, and SSAs in identifying and meeting their R&D requirements. As a result, the IP Research & Development Project Office serves as the SSA's liaison to S&T and assists the ESS by tracking the progress of its technology gaps, R&D initiatives, and initiatives of other sectors that impact first responders.

The ES SSA coordinates the development of the sector R&D planning component of the SSP and Sector Annual Report so that these documents reflect the sector's R&D investment priorities. Coordination among the GCC and SCC, IP, S&T, and SSA is critical to ensure the R&D information in the SSP and SAR is comprehensive and reflects the needs of the sector. This information is reported to Congress on an annual basis through the National Annual Report.

7.2 Sector Research and Development Requirements

At the Federal level, the R&D process outlined in the NIPP assists the sector to identify and articulate strategic R&D requirements and to facilitate effective and efficient coordination with S&T and other divisions. Sector needs are aligned with expertise in academia, research and analysis centers, S&T Centers of Excellence, and the private sector to facilitate the development of solutions. The five phases of the NIPP R&D Requirements Process include:

- Identification and articulation of CIKR sector gaps in operational capabilities;

- IP collection and analysis;

- Validation of the gaps through steering group reviews;

- Solution identification through available providers; and

- Execution and implementation of the desired product or process.

R&D requirements are guided based on how the sector identifies and prioritizes its protective needs. As discussed in chapter 5, there is an organized approach that the ESS utilizes to identify and prioritize protective needs, which in turn informs the sector about R&D gaps that may exist. The sector first looks to the National Preparedness Guidelines, which establish a vision for preparedness and a systematic methodology for conducting needs assessments and prioritizing preparedness efforts across the Nation that translate to the national goals. Additionally, the NCIP R&D Plan outlines three strategic goals that guide Federal R&D investment decisions and also provide a coordinated approach to the overall Federal research program. R&D projects for CIKR protection that support the national strategic goals generally fall into seven R&D themes. These themes provide an organizing framework for the SSA to specify capabilities needed to satisfy CIKR protection needs, which lead to the development of corresponding requirements. As noted from tables 7-1, 7-2, and 7-3 below, the national priorities are aligned with the National Preparedness Guidelines, the National R&D strategic goals, and the seven organizing themes.

Table 7-1: National Preparedness Priorities

National Preparedness Priorities
· Strengthening preparedness planning, training, and exercises
· Strengthening IED deterrence, prevention, protection, and response capabilities
· Strengthening information-sharing capabilities and communication interoperability
· Improving medical readiness through strengthening medical surge capability and mass prophylaxis
· Strengthening preventive radiological and nuclear detection capabilities
· Strengthening CBRNE capabilities

Table 7-2: NCIP National Strategic Goals

NCIP National Strategic Goals for CIKR Protection
· CIKR common operating pictures
· Next generation Internet architecture with built-in security
· Resilient, self-diagnosing, self-healing infrastructure systems

Table 7-3: CIKR R&D Themes

CIKR R&D Themes
· Detection and sensor systems
· Protection and prevention
· Entry and access portals
· Insider threats
· Analysis and decision support systems
· Response, recovery, and reconstitution
· New and emerging threats and vulnerabilities
· Advanced infrastructure architectures and system designs
· Human and social issues

Another mechanism to identify sector R&D requirements is through S&T. S&T engages all levels of government, industry, academia, and ESS partners in collaborative efforts to identify and remedy areas of vulnerability through research, development, testing, and evaluation of technologies.

Cybersecurity and Communications R&D Requirements

As referenced in chapter 1, with the increasing interconnected nature and inherent complexity of IT and cyber systems, cyber issues are a major concern for the sector. A lack of standards, combined with variations in organization, diversity of assets, availability of resources, and other factors create a very diverse and dynamic cyber landscape. Although some similarities exist, first responders use cyber systems differently in their daily activities.

Many ESS activities are vulnerable to cyber attack. These activities include emergency response operations, medical dispatch, database management, biometrics, telecommunications, and electronic security systems. The sector uses the Internet widely to provide information and receive alerts, warnings, and threats relevant to the ESS. Additionally, users who rely on the Internet for monitoring CAD systems, such as the 9-1-1 Dispatch Systems, risk degradation of response capability if connectivity is lost.

A major focus of the ESS Cyber Security Working Group (CSWG) is identifying cybersecurity and communication technology requirements for the sector. The ESS CSWG, in coordination with the MS-ISAC, works to identify emerging cyber threats and provide coordination and oversight of those requirements.

In addition to the sector-specific cyber issues addressed through the ESS Working Group, the ES SSA participates in DHS CSCSWG to gain the integrated, cross-sector cybersecurity perspective needed to address the mutual concerns and issues across sectors. This cross-sector perspective facilitates information sharing about various cybersecurity concerns, such as common vulnerabilities and protective measures, and leverages functional cyber expertise in a comprehensive forum. Managing cyber risk and securing cyberspace is an issue that cuts across the Nation's CIKR and the CSCSWG serves to ensure effective coordination to address cybersecurity in a collaborative manner with all of the sectors.

A major emphasis of the ESS is the NIMS mandate for interoperability and compatibility of first responder communications systems. The vast majority of first responders are limited in their ability to communicate and collaborate with command support teams and other responding organizations during an incident. A communications framework that enables the interoperability of disparate systems and the ability to interconnect legacy systems and new systems is required. R&D projects within the Interoperability and Cybersecurity Capstone IPTs develop solutions to improve interoperability and information sharing. Technology requirements recently developed by these IPTs include:

- Wireless technologies that offer secure delivery of critical information used by public safety, emergency preparedness, and law enforcement;
- Real-time data processing and visualization technology that enables on-demand management, analysis and visualization of information in multiple forms and from diverse, distributed sources;
- Threat Dissemination Standards for sharing information within sectors and across sectors to defeat terrorist threats;
- Data fusion technologies for fusing data from multiple sensors to support threat identification and decision analysis; and
- Law enforcement and Intelligence Sensor fusion technologies.

The IAB also identified similar requirements related to cyber technology, including CAD-to-CAD interface, personal wireless networks incorporating specific capabilities, and personal Bluetooth® like radio interface.

Although many of the issues faced by the ESS are aligned with new and emerging threats and vulnerabilities to our communications systems, there are also challenges that currently exist in the manner in which government can communicate effectively with the American public. For example, the IPAWS has been mandated by Executive Order to ensure public alert and warning messages also reach a growing population that has difficulty in understanding English. Another segment of our population that must be reached in times of crisis consists of those individuals with hearing or sight disabilities.

The ability of the ES SSA to track R&D initiatives across all sectors is enhanced through coordination with the IP R&D Project Office and active participation by the sector on S&T Capstone IPTs, and through engaging the IAB. Additionally, the sector partnership enables close coordination with the GCC and SCC to facilitate the identification of R&D activities external to DHS, including private sector activities. The ESS GCC and SCC provide oversight for the Sector R&D plan, and activities and unmet requirements are tracked through the ESS R&D Working Group. The R&D activities and unmet requirements are reported in the SAR and subsequently included in the NAR.

7.3 Sector R&D Plan

The major emphasis of the ESS R&D plan is to ensure the CIKR R&D needs of the sector are addressed at some level of government or within the private sector. There are numerous R&D projects conducted at the Federal level that impact the sector. The challenge is to differentiate between those that are operational and those that enhance the protection of the sector from a CIKR perspective. As discussed earlier, a major R&D challenge for the ES SSA is to remain abreast of the current Federal program initiatives sourced within the S&T Capstone IPTs and communicate the information to the GCC and SCC. Once informed of the Federal R&D projects, the GCC and SCC review the comprehensive list of projects and determine if technology requirements exist that are not addressed at the Federal level.

Additionally, even though ESS requirements are submitted at the Federal level by State, local, tribal, and territorial entities within the sector, there still exist numerous requirements and activities that may be conducted at the regional, State, or local level. Through ongoing collaboration with the GCC and SCC, a crosswalk of activities at all levels of government is conducted to identify R&D areas of duplication, overlap, and omission.

Numerous methods inform the sector of ESS R&D requirements and projects. One method is the quarterly Sector Initiatives Call, which collects current and future R&D requirements and programs from sector partners, then provides a report to the GCC and SCC. The sector receives ongoing updates of R&D projects conducted at the Federal level through meetings, postings on the HSIN-CS/ESS portal and the Resource Knowledge Base, and annual reporting in the SAR. The sector engages the IAB, which identifies R&D priorities that are communicated to the sector through the IAB annual report. Additionally, sector partners address priority requirements for the sector as participating members of various S&T and IAB committees.

To ensure a comprehensive approach to CIKR R&D activities, the sector established an ES R&D Working Group (RDWG). The mission of the working group is to:

- Coordinate the identification and prioritization of CIKR R&D requirements;

- Capture R&D activities at all levels of government and the private sector, to ensure that each need is met through the creation of a new product or the adaptation of an existing product;

- Serve as the conduit between the GCC and SCC, DHS S&T, IAB, and other agencies to communicate R&D requirements and activities;

- Facilitate the development of ESS CIKR R&D un-met requirements, as necessary; and

- Develop the annual R&D reporting component of the SAR.

The RDWG works closely with IPTs, other S&T components (i.e., Commercialization; Interagency Coordination; First Responder Technologies; and Command, Control, and Interoperability), and a number of sector partners that are involved with R&D work.

As reported in the 2009 Sector Annual Report, the sector submitted technology requirements to S&T based on input from sector partners. From these technology requirements, the sector identified seven capability gaps (see Appendix 5) of which two were approved, four required further review by the ESS RDWG, and one was transferred to the National Institute for Homeland Security. One of the approved capability gaps regarding emergency services and private vehicle operation within a large, life-threatening toxic vapor chlorine cloud was developed by the ES SSA in collaboration with the Chemical Sector and TSA.

7.4 Sector R&D Management Processes

The ES SSA, in collaboration with the ES GCC and SCC, coordinates oversight of the R&D activities within the sector. The ESS RDWG is responsible for monitoring, conducting R&D activities, assessing impact on sector goals, and updating the ESS R&D plan, as required. Due to the expansiveness of the sector, R&D requirements are identified and managed through a broad-based approach that incorporates activities at all levels of government and the private sector. Networking and information sharing among sector partners is critical to maintain awareness of R&D activities. Ultimately, close collaboration with the ES GCC and SCC provides the review and guidance to evaluate and pursue projects that enhance the effectiveness of the first responders. As the ESS RDWG fully matures, it is expected that the sector's accounting of R&D requirements and activities will improve as will the reporting of activities to the GCC and SCC at the national level.

8. Managing and Coordinating Sector-Specific Agency Responsibilities

This section describes how the SSA will administer its responsibilities as the sector lead for coordinating protective programs and resilience strategies in partnership with CIKR stakeholders. In addition, this section details how the SSA will manage SSP development, maintenance, and implementation; the processes used for identifying and managing budgetary and resource needs for CIKR protection and resilience; and the processes used for establishing and tracking SSP Implementation Milestones. Finally, this section describes how the sector is implementing the NIPP sector partnership model, describes sector training and education initiatives, and discusses how the sector protects and shares information among sector partners, across sectors, and with other relevant stakeholders.

8.1 Program Management Approach

DHS assigned the National Protection and Programs Directorate (NPPD) the responsibility of strengthening national risk management efforts for critical infrastructure. NPPD defines and synchronizes homeland security policy within DHS and across the Federal Government as well as across State, local, tribal, territorial, and private sector CIKR partners. Within NPPD, IP leads the coordinated effort to reduce the risk to the 18 CIKR sectors and strengthen national preparedness, timely response, and rapid recovery in the event of an attack, natural disaster, or other emergency. Within IP, the Sector-Specific Agency Executive Management Office (SSA EMO) is assigned the responsibility for implementing the NIPP framework for six CIKR sectors: Chemical, Commercial Facilities, Critical Manufacturing, Dams, Emergency Services, and Nuclear. The success of SSA EMO is highly dependent on integration with other IP divisions and associated projects within DHS, as well as on ongoing engagement with government and private sector partners.

Each SSA is ultimately reliant on strong public-private partnership and coordination for the implementation of meaningful programs to reduce all-hazards risk across the six CIKR sectors. To execute its mission, SSA EMO has established five primary program areas that support the implementation of the SSPs and NIPP risk management framework, and build and mature SSA functionality.

These program areas contain cross-sector and sector-specific initiatives that allow SSA EMO to manage the overall process for building partnerships, and for implementing the SSP by leveraging CIKR protection expertise, relationships, and resource investments, prioritized as a result of effective risk management:

- **Planning and Project Integration:** Effective planning and project integration enable individual SSAs, through SSA EMO, to build and sustain partnerships both internal and external to DHS; synchronize and communicate common objectives, responsibilities, and initiatives across the six IP SSAs; readily share relevant cross-sector information; and better understand the needs and requirements of sector partners.

- **Education and Training:** To raise security awareness and increase the cadre of trained individuals across SSA EMO sectors, SSA EMO has collaborated with sector partners to develop a wide range of training and protection awareness initiatives. These programs help to raise the security bar within CIKR sectors and provide easy-to-use, accessible tools that enable sector partners to share best practices across the entire range of CIKR protection activities.

- **Partnership and Information Sharing:** The cornerstone of effective CIKR protection, resilience planning, and program implementation is the voluntary public-private partnership established under CIPAC. SSAs work closely with government and private sector partners to develop an inclusive critical infrastructure protection and resilience strategy that is reflective of sector needs and priorities. In addition, this partnership facilitates efficient information sharing across government, as well as between government and the private sector, sustaining educated decision making for the implementation of programs and initiatives.

- **Exercises and Incident Management:** The SSAs are responsible for providing government decision makers and other sector partners with a clear and accurate picture of the potential or real impact of an incident to the sector and of the potential cross-sector, regional, and international consequences resulting from the incident. The SSA is responsible for carrying out the following core incident management functions:

  - **Situational Awareness:** Monitor information flow and threats to gain and maintain awareness of an incident or potential incident;

  - **Analyses and Assessments:** Analyze and assess incoming situational and tactical information, and place it in a proper sector-specific context for DHS and other key decision makers to support greater understanding of sector risks. The ES SSA also provides guidance to senior leadership for prioritization, protection, resilience, and recovery activities associated with an incident;

  - **Information Sharing:** Participate in robust multi-directional incident information sharing with sector partners to ensure timely, clear, and pertinent information is provided to support decision making; and

  - **Requests for Information:** Provide sector-specific information to the IP Contingency Planning and Incident Management Division incident management cell and the NICC in response to requests for information from CIKR stakeholders.

- **Assessment and Mitigation:** The SSA works with partners to develop sector-specific protective programs designed to deter, mitigate, or neutralize potential attacks. As the risk landscape changes, the SSA works with Federal, State, local, tribal, and territorial governments and private sector partners to develop and implement effective practices that build resilience within its sector.

8.2 Processes and Responsibilities

8.2.1 Sector-Specific Plan Maintenance and Update

The primary planning document for the sector, the SSP provides the framework for NIPP implementation across the sector. As a core competency of the SSA, the SSP is developed jointly by the SSA, GCC, and SCC, as well as by other partners with key interests or expertise appropriate to the ESS, including State, local, tribal, and territorial governments and practitioners. The ESS partners tailor the SSP to address the unique characteristics and risk landscapes of the sector while maintaining a balanced and flexible approach that reflects the status and requirements of the sector. The ES SSA updates its SSP as necessary and required by the sector, and leads the revision of the document every three years in conjunction with the update of the NIPP Base Plan.

The ES SSA works with its GCC, SCC, State representatives, subject matter experts, and others, as appropriate, to assess requirements for updating and amending the SSP (based on changes to sector priorities, NIPP PMO guidance, etc.) and to draft the revised SSP. The ES SSA strives to ensure that the finalized SSP is a cooperative and comprehensive planning document that accurately captures the sector landscape, sets forth commonly agreed on sector goals and priorities, accurately describes sector resilience initiatives and protective programs, and outlines criteria for measuring progress toward risk reduction. The GCC and SCC, as well as State, local, tribal, and territorial representatives, subject matter experts, and SSA EMO and IP leadership review the document and provide substantive input. Comments and changes are adjudicated, and revised drafts are issued. The ES SSA drafts the document, coordinates all comments, and maintains full version control.

8.2.2 Sector-Specific Plan Implementation Milestones

The implementation milestones set forth in the SSP enable sector partners, the ES SSA, and DHS to gauge progress toward verifying, validating, and realizing the goals and objectives as defined in chapter 1 of the SSP. In accordance with sector reporting requirements, the ESS has the opportunity to update sector goals and objectives annually, with a thorough review completed triennially concurrent with the SSP rewrite. By incorporating this process into the SSP rewrite, it ensures that the ES SSA has full engagement and buy-in from sector partners. These goals and objectives inform the development and implementation of sector-wide programs, and enable the ESS to implement appropriate protective activities.

Table 8-1: Emergency Services Sector-Specific Plan Milestones Aligned with the NIPP Risk Management Framework

Chevron	Milestone
Set goals and objectives	• In collaboration with the ES SCC and GCC, revised the sector profile, the ES mission, and the description of the sector's disciplines, goals, and objectives.
Identify assets, systems, and networks	• Continue to collaborate with sector partners to review current data collection methods, such as ACAMS, NCAD, and TCL, and to identify and discuss future potential databases. • Collaborate with IICD to identify technological developments to improve or modify current data collection methods.
Assess risks	• Continue to encourage stakeholder and sector partners' involvement with the ESSAT to support sector-wide risk management efforts. • Participate in ESS Risk Assessment Workshop with practitioners from across the country with GCC and SCC representation. • Further engage the newly developed RAWG to discuss risk assessments of critical elements in the ESS and its subcomponents.
Prioritize	• Collaborate with sector partners to prioritize key risk mitigation activities on an annual basis. • Promote the use of ESSAT sector wide.
Implement protective programs and resilience strategies	• Continue to collaborate with sector partners to ensure that data collection is accurate, cost-effective, and efficient in order to monitor protective programs implementation. • Continue to moderate the ESS ISWG. • Continue to moderate the ESS Information Requirements Sub-Working Group. • Participate in the annual National Level Exercise.
Measure effectiveness	• Provide metrics data for key risk mitigation activities to NIPP Measurement and Reporting Office on a yearly basis.

8.2.3 Sector-Specific Agency Responsibilities

HSPD-7 requires SSAs to provide an annual report to DHS detailing the sector's efforts "to identify, prioritize, and coordinate the protection of critical infrastructure and key resources" applicable to the sector. The information provided in the annual report allows DHS to make informed decisions related to allocation of scarce resources to support the sector's priorities, requirements, and efforts. The SCC is an active participant in the development of the annual report and ensures that the document comprehensively reports the sector's priorities and requirements. The SSA submits the annual report to DHS no later than July 1 of each calendar year. Subsequently, DHS incorporates the information into the National Annual Report. Major elements of the Sector Annual Report include:

- Priorities and goals for CIKR protection and associated gaps;
- Sector-specific requirements for CIKR protection activities and programs based on risk and need; and
- Projected CIKR-related resource requirements for the sector.

SSA EMO leadership meets regularly with IP and DHS senior leadership to discuss the status of various SSA initiatives; this includes formal IP quarterly report briefings that track budget, acquisition, personnel, and SSA Management Project execution. These internal reporting and management mechanisms better enable SSA EMO to plan for and meet the needs of the ES SSA and the sector, and to address DHS, congressional, and White House reporting requirements.

8.2.4 Resources and Budgets

The ES SSA is responsible for leading the effort to coordinate protection and resilience initiatives and strategy across the sector. The first step for the SSA in the risk-based resource allocation process is to coordinate with sector partners, including the SCC and GCC, to accurately determine sector priorities, program requirements, and funding needs for CIKR protection. Further complicating the resource allocation process are the diverse disciplines that comprise the ESS. These disciplines encompass numerous networks and systems and make identification of specific protective measures extremely complex. The SSA communicates information about existing CIKR protection-related programs and outstanding requirements to DHS through the Sector Annual Report.

DHS develops and shares resource allocation recommendations based on the national priorities identified in the NIPP, the National Annual Report, and sector priorities developed in support of the SSP. An analysis of cost-effectiveness and potential risk reduction informs these recommendations.

It is important to note that numerous Federal, State, local, tribal, and territorial governments, as well as trade organizations and individual practitioners, manage and implement protective programs vital to the sector. Accordingly, it is beyond the SSA's capability and scope of mission to account for all resources devoted to CIKR protection in the ES Sector, or to direct allocation of resources beyond its control. Sector stakeholders as a whole take advantage of grant funding offered through DHS' Grants Program Directorate, as well as other Federal agency grant programs.

SSA EMO manages resourcing and budget for the ES SSA and works within the IP budget process to submit personnel and program requirements in accordance with the needs of each of the IP SSAs for which it is responsible. The ES SSA is responsible for outlining SSA personnel needs, sector-specific programmatic priorities, and associated cost estimates in alignment with overarching SSA EMO and sector goals, objectives, and priorities. SSA EMO leadership manages the ES SSA's budget, and budget allocation decisions are made based on the stated priorities of each SSA EMO SSA and through a consultative process between SSA EMO and IP Leadership.

SSA requests are submitted as part of the IP budget, which is incorporated into DHS' annual budget submission to the Office of Management and Budget (OMB).

The Federal resource allocation process is as follows:

- February–July: IP, in conjunction with other DHS offices and divisions as appropriate, develops the recommended DHS budget requests for ESS-related expenditures;
- July–September: Sector Annual Reports are analyzed and the National Annual Report is published on September 1; and

- September–November: IP and the SSAs, through DHS channels, work with OMB to remedy any gaps or shortcomings to NIPP-related funding focusing on ensuring funding of programs associated with nationally critical assets, systems, networks, or functions.

8.2.5 Training and Education

Successful implementation of the national risk management framework relies on building and maintaining individual and organizational CIKR protection expertise. Training, education, and outreach in a variety of areas are necessary to achieve and sustain this level of expertise and, as such, are a key focus of the ES SSA.

The critical nature of services that the ESS disciplines provide to the community requires participation in accredited formal academic programs, professional certification programs, and technical training programs. ESS personnel possess expert technical skills and knowledge requiring baseline certification training in order to safely and effectively perform in their area of expertise. Beyond initial training, recertification training is required in most disciplines and sub-capabilities. ESS personnel must regularly practice the skills either through participation in skill labs, drills, seminars, classrooms, workshops, or through functional/full-level exercises to maintain competency. Ongoing professional continuing education is also a crucial component to ensuring that ESS personnel are prepared to carry out their mission. Attendance at annual professional conferences provides an avenue for ESS personnel to receive further education related to best practices, new technology, and other topics to enhance their emergency response capabilities. Several well-known training institutions such as the Emergency Management Institute, the Office of Domestic Preparedness, the National Fire Academy, and the National Domestic Preparedness Consortium provide extensive training opportunities, often free of cost to sector personnel.

Also available to ESS partners are training programs related to performing risk assessments, risk management, cost-benefit analysis, cybersecurity strategies, and related concepts. Of equal importance to the ESS partners is awareness training specific to current threats and correspondence courses and independent study programs related to CIKR protection initiatives.

To foster preparedness and increase effective response during an incident, the ES SSA works with the sector to develop and participate in sector-specific as well as national cross-sector exercises. These initiatives provide critically important lessons learned for the state of preparedness, information sharing, and incident management procedures and protocols. Examples of cross-sector exercises in which the SSA has participated include National Level Exercises, Cyber Storm, and Dams Sector Exercises.

Even though ESS partners aggressively pursue a variety of individual and organizational education and training activities, the ES SSA continues to coordinate with the sector to identify gaps in training and examine ways to meet educational needs.

8.3 Implementing the Partnership Model

Chapter 1 of the SSP describes the specific organizational entities and participants involved in the coordinated development and implementation of a robust and comprehensive strategy for the sector. The SSA works with these partners to support initiatives targeting specific disciplines and issues of concern, as well as broader initiatives and strategies that foster partnership, coordination, information sharing, and risk management across the sector. The NIPP sector partnership model is the overarching framework within which the broad CIKR partnership operates.

DHS established CIPAC in 2006 to facilitate effective coordination among Federal, State, local, tribal, and territorial governments, and between government and the private sector. CIPAC provides a forum that allows CIKR partners to engage in a broad range of critical infrastructure protection and resilience activities. CIPAC membership includes:

- Sector Coordinating Councils are self-formed groups within the sector that serve as the government's principal point of entry into each sector for infrastructure protection activities and issues;

- Government Coordinating Councils are complementary to the SCCs, formed as the government counterpart for each sector to enable inter-agency coordination;

- The CIKR Cross-Sector Council encompasses the PCIS. Membership of the PCIS includes the chairpersons from each of the SCCs;

- The Government Cross-Sector Council is comprised of two sub-councils: the NIPP Federal Senior Leadership Council and the SLTTGCC;

- The State, Local, Tribal, and Territorial Government Coordinating Council serves as the forum to ensure that State, local, tribal, and territorial governments are fully integrated into the CIKR protection process and can actively coordinate across their jurisdictions and with the Federal Government on CIKR protection guidance, strategies, and programs;

- The NIPP Federal Senior Leadership Council, composed of leadership from each SSA, drives enhanced communication and coordination among Federal departments and agencies; and

- The Regional Consortium Coordinating Council brings together regional representatives and organizations to enable CIKR protection coordination across geographical areas and sectors.

Additional information on key sector partners and councils, such as the SCC and GCC, is available in chapter 1 of this document. The ongoing communication and coordination enabled by this broad public-private partnership are critical to the ES SSA's mission to manage its responsibilities for leading the unified effort to manage risks to the sector.

8.4 Information Sharing and Protection

8.4.1 Information Sharing

Development and maintenance of a robust public-private partnership requires routine and comprehensive information sharing among all sector partners. The ability to share information efficiently with sector partners, the Federal Government, as well as external stakeholders is vital to efficient steady-state infrastructure protection activity, as well as effective incident management. Although the GCC and SCC provide channels for Federal Government representatives to coordinate with sector stakeholders, additional means of communication are necessary for sharing information between the Federal Government and the ESS. As discussed in this SSP, DHS provides numerous channels through which it disseminates information to and receives information from State and local governments and ESS members.

8.4.1.1 National Infrastructure Coordinating Center

The NICC serves as IP's focal point for event situational awareness across the 18 CIKR sectors during normal operations and incident management activities. The NICC is both an operational component of IP and a watch operations element of the DHS NOC. The NICC operates 24 hours a day, 7 days a week, 365 days a year to facilitate coordination and information sharing within CIKR sectors. The NICC produces consolidated CIKR reports for incorporation into the Federal Interagency DHS Common Operating Picture. During an incident, the NICC provides situation reports to the SSAs through the Executive Notification System (ENS). The SSAs, in turn, contact their respective CIKR partners to develop impact assessments.

8.4.1.2 Information Sharing and Analysis Centers

Information-sharing and communication mechanisms, known as Information Sharing and Analysis Centers (ISACs), exist in some sectors to collect, analyze, and disseminate threat and security-related information in a timely manner. The ISACs most relevant to ESS include the EMR-ISAC and the MS-ISAC.

The EMR-ISAC, located at the USFA in Maryland, has the responsibility to disseminate critical infrastructure protection and resilience information to stakeholders within ESS. ESS stakeholders register to receive information, through the secure portals of **www.interactive.dhs.gov.** The products distributed by EMR-ISAC contain emergent, actionable information regarding threats and vulnerabilities to support effective advanced preparedness, protection, and mitigation activities. Additionally, due to the dependencies and interdependencies of ESS with other sectors, the EMR-ISAC continually strives to foster a cross-sector information-sharing environment. The SSA coordinates with the EMR-ISAC to align and coordinate initiatives across the sector and to improve information sharing and connectivity. This collaborative effort accomplishes the following:

- Improvement in the ability to assess reliably the status of ESS departments and agencies during and after a disaster;

- Enhanced dissemination of sector "ground truth" information during a crisis;

- Greater sector participation in an information-sharing network; and

- Opportunities to acquire an understanding of sector needs and concerns that may necessitate an adjustment of CIKR protection, research, and development actions.

Established in January 2003, the MS-ISAC is a voluntary and collaborative effort among the States and local governments to facilitate communication regarding cyber and critical infrastructure readiness and response efforts. MS-ISAC is managed by the New York State Office of Cyber Security and Critical Infrastructure Coordination and has been recognized by DHS for its proactive role in bringing the States together. The MS-ISAC provides the ESS a common mechanism for raising the level of cybersecurity readiness and response within the sector and provides a central resource for gathering information from the sector regarding cyber threats to critical infrastructure.

8.4.1.3 Emergency Services Sector Information Sharing Working Group

The ESS ISWG supports the sector's critical infrastructure protection mission-related information-sharing priorities with the CIKR sector partnership and is congruent with the DHS responsibility to foster information sharing internally within DHS, horizontally within the U.S. Government, and among law enforcement and intelligence agencies and sector partners. The ESS ISWG seeks to ensure information sharing within DHS, across Federal, State, local, tribal and territorial governments, and with private sector partners, law enforcement, and intelligence agencies. The ESS ISWG exists to review, refine, and develop information-sharing mechanisms related to information collection, storage, dissemination, and security. The ESS ISWG sector partnership identified and prioritized the information-sharing processes and activities required for critical infrastructure protection missions. Specifically, the ESS ISWG provides the platform for expansion of information-sharing policies and the coordinated development of core capabilities and enhanced ESS mission-related information-sharing and protection processes.

8.4.1.4 Homeland Security Information Network-Critical Sectors

The HSIN-CS is the primary technology used to support information exchange within the CIKR information-sharing environment. Its objectives are to generate effective risk management decisions, and to encourage collaboration and coordination on plans, strategies, protective measures, and response/recovery efforts between government, operators, and owners in the public and private sectors. HSIN-CS focuses on the protection of CIKR assets through information sharing focusing on the core CIKR information-sharing processes that include alerts, warnings and notifications; suspicious activity reporting; data management; and incident and routine collaboration.

8.4.1.5 Homeland Security Information Network-Emergency Management

The Homeland Security Information Network-Emergency Management (HSIN-EM) is the national hub for all HSIN members that have emergency management responsibilities, i.e., first responders, response planners, fire, and police assets. Unlike HSIN-CS, HSIN-EM has an operational focus that is reflected in the subsites created for the various disciplines within the sector.

In recognition of the increasing threat to the sector's cyber assets, the ESS supports several initiatives and partnerships that increase the sector's ability to deter, mitigate, and respond to cyber events. These partnerships allow sector representatives to communicate threat information to other stakeholders, as well as develop sector-specific and cross-sector best practices.

United States Computer Emergency Readiness Team: A public/private partnership established in 2003 to protect the Nation's Internet infrastructure, US-CERT coordinates defenses against and responses to cyber attacks across the Nation. As part of this responsibility, US-CERT interacts with Federal agencies, industry, the research community, State and local governments, and others to disseminate reasoned and actionable cybersecurity information to the public.

Multi-State Information Sharing and Analysis Center: MS-ISAC is a collaborative State and local government-focused cybersecurity entity that enhances cyber threat prevention, protection, response, and recovery nationwide. The MS-ISAC's primary objectives are to:

• Provide two-way sharing of information and early warnings on cybersecurity threats;

• Provide a process for gathering and disseminating information on cybersecurity incidents;

• Promote awareness of the interdependencies between cyber and physical critical infrastructure as well as between and among the different sectors;

• Coordinate training and awareness; and

• Ensure that all necessary parties are vested partners in this effort.

Cross-Sector Cyber Security Working Group: CSCSWG provides a forum to bring government and the private sector together to collaboratively address risk across all CIKR sectors under the CIPAC. The CSCSWG addresses a wide variety of cybersecurity issues and enables comprehensive planning and sharing of information across the community of interested stakeholders.

Critical Infrastructure Warning Information Network: The Critical Infrastructure Warning Information Network (CWIN) is the critical, survivable network connecting DHS with the vital sectors that are essential in restoring the Nation's infrastructure during incidents of national significance. CWIN provides voice and data connectivity using Voice Over Internet Protocol phones, thin client computing devices, and, in select locations, videoconferencing capabilities. In addition, CWIN connects EOCs of the fifty States and the District of Columbia to the NOC. CWIN's backbone is used to provide classified connectivity between DHS, the States, and select law enforcement sites via HSIN.

Emergency Services Sector Cybersecurity Working Group: As a subgroup of the ISWG, the ESS CSWG addresses cyber concerns faced by the sector. Consisting of representatives from both the SCC and GCC, the ESS Cybersecurity Working Group facilitates planning efforts, information sharing, and R&D cyber initiatives among sector stakeholders.

8.4.2 Protecting Information

In many cases, information used by DHS and its sector partners to effectively manage risk and secure the Nation's critical infrastructure contains sensitive business and proprietary information. As a result, information protection is a significant concern for those CIKR partners that must supply such information. DHS takes the need to protect this information extremely seriously, and will do so to the maximum extent allowed by law.

Information held by the SSA and by sector partners is designated as classified, sensitive but unclassified, or open according to corresponding distribution conditions and classification guidelines. Although the Federal Government maintains a preference for full transparency, the security sensitive nature of much of the information obtained by the ES SSA and its government partners may require classified or restricted access and protection from general public disclosure.

Pursuant to the Critical Infrastructure Information Act of 2002, the Protected Critical Infrastructure Information (PCII) Program was created to protect from public disclosure, to the maximum extent permitted by law, sensitive and proprietary critical infrastructure information submitted to DHS, provided this information satisfies the requirements of the act . The DHS PCII Program Office within IP manages this program.

The rules governing the program are located in title 6, part 29 of the Code of Federal Regulations. General information on the program, including instructions on how to properly submit information in compliance with it, can be found on the DHS Web site at **www.dhs.gov/pcii**. The PCII Program and similar information protection initiatives developed by DHS help address the concerns of many owners and operators who wish to keep sensitive, proprietary, business, and security-related information confidential. As a result, owners and operators are more willing to share information with DHS through the PCII Program.

DHS has exercised its authority under section 871 of the Homeland Security Act to exempt the CIPAC from the Federal Advisory Committee Act.[1] This ensures that the CIPAC members can discuss sensitive security issues without the risk that these discussions could become public and jeopardize security. The CIPAC can meet as a whole, or in the form of joint committees specific to a particular sector.

[1] Federal Register (FR) 14930 (March 24, 2006)

Appendix 1: List of Acronyms and Abbreviations

ARC	American Red Cross
ASPR	Office of the Assistant Secretary for Preparedness and Response
BMAP	Bomb-Making Materials Awareness Program
BZP	Buffer Zone Plan
BZPP	Buffer Zone Protection Program
C4ISR	Command, Control, Communications, Computers, Intelligence, Surveillance, and Reconnaissance
CAD	Computer-Aided Dispatch
CBRNE	Chemical, Biological, Radiological, Nuclear, and High-Yield Explosives
CCCIIT	Command-Control-Cyber-Intelligence-Information Technology
CFDI	Critical Foreign Dependencies Initiative
CIKR	Critical Infrastructure and Key Resources
CII	Critical Infrastructure Information
CIPAC	Critical Infrastructure Partnership Advisory Council
COG	Continuity of Government
COGCON	Continuity of Government Condition
COOP	Continuity of Operations
CS&C	Office of Cyber Security and Communications
CSCSWG	Cross-Sector Cyber Security Working Group
CV	Common Vulnerability
DHS	Department of Homeland Security
DOC	Department of Commerce
DoD	Department of Defense
DOT	Department of Transportation
DPA	Defense Production Act
ECIP	Enhanced Critical Infrastructure Protection

EM	Emergency Management
EMAC	Emergency Management Assistance Compact
EMI	Emergency Management Institute
EMO	Executive Management Office
EMR-ISAC	Emergency Management and Response Information Sharing and Analysis Center
EMS	Emergency Medical Services
EOC	Emergency Operations Center
EOD	Explosive Ordnance Disposal
EPCRA	Emergency Planning and Community Right-to-Know Act
ES	Emergency Services
ESF	Emergency Support Function
ESS	Emergency Services Sector
ESSAT	Emergency Services Self Assessment Tool
FAZD	National Center for Foreign Animal and Zoonotic Disease Defense
FBI	Federal Bureau of Investigation
FCO	Federal Coordinating Officer
FEMA	Federal Emergency Management Agency
FIPS	Federal Information Processing Standard
FOUO	For Official Use Only
FRC	Federal Resource Coordinator
FSLC	Federal Senior Leadership Council
GCC	Government Coordinating Council
GPD	Grants Programs Directorate
HAZMAT	Hazardous Materials
HHS	Department of Health and Human Services
HITRAC	Homeland Infrastructure Threat and Risk Analysis Center
HSAS	Homeland Security Advisory System
HSC	Homeland Security Council
HSIN	Homeland Security Information Network
HSPD	Homeland Security Presidential Directive
IAB	Inter-Agency Board
IACP	International Association of Chiefs of Police
IAEM	International Association of Emergency Managers
IAFC	International Association of Fire Chiefs
IAFF	International Association of Fire Fighters

ICE	Immigration and Customs Enforcement
ICS	Incident Command System
IDW	Infrastructure Data Warehouse
IED	Improvised Explosive Device
IICD	Infrastructure Information Collection Division
IICS	Infrastructure Information Collection System
IM&C	Information Management and Communications
IP	Office of Infrastructure Protection
IPT	Integrated Product Team
IRAPP	Infrastructure Risk Analysis Partnership Program
ISAC	Information Sharing and Analysis Center
IST	Infrastructure Survey Tool
ISWG	Information Sharing Working Group
IT	Information Technology
JFO	Joint Field Office
JOC	Joint Operations Center
KCI	Kentucky Critical Infrastructure Protection Institute Program
LEAs	Law Enforcement Agencies
LEPC	Local Emergency Planning Committee
MAA	Mutual-Aid Agreement
MACS	Multiagency Coordination Systems
MJBPP	Multi-Jurisdiction Bombing Prevention Plan
MMRS	Metropolitan Medical Response System
MOA	Memorandum of Agreement
MOU	Memorandum of Understanding
MRO	Measurement and Reporting Office
MS-ISAC	Multi-State Information Sharing and Analysis Center
NADB	National Asset Database
NASEMSO	National Association of State EMS Officials
NCC	National Coordinating Center for Communications
NCIPP	National Critical Infrastructure Prioritization Program
NCS	National Communications System
NCSD	National Cyber Security Division
NCTC	National Counterterrorism Center
NDMS	National Disaster Medical System

NEF	National Essential Function
NEMA	National Emergency Management Association
NFPA	National Fire Protection Association
NGB	National Guard Bureau
NGO	Nongovernmental Organization
NHTSA	National Highway Traffic Safety Administration
NIC	NIMS Integration Center
NICC	National Infrastructure Coordinating Center
NIMS	National Incident Management System
NIMSCAST	NIMS Capability Assessment Support Tool
NIOSH	National Institute for Occupational Safety and Health
NIPP	National Infrastructure Protection Plan
NOAA	National Oceanic and Atmospheric Administration
NOC	National Operations Center
NPG	National Preparedness Guidelines
NRCC	National Response Coordination Center
NRF	National Response Framework
NSA	National Sheriffs' Association
NS/EP	National Security and Emergency Preparedness
NSSE	National Special Security Event
NWS	National Weather Service
OBP	Office for Bombing Prevention
OEC	Office of Emergency Communications
OEM	Office of Emergency Management
OHA	Office of Health Affairs
OMB	Office of Management and Budget
OSHA	Occupational Safety and Health Administration
OSTP	Office of Science and Technology Policy
PACER	Preparedness and Catastrophic Event Response
PALMS	Private Asset and Logistics Management System
PCII	Protected Critical Infrastructure Information
PCIS	Partnership for Critical Infrastructure Security
PDA	Preliminary Damage Assessment
PFO	Principal Federal Official
PHMSA	Pipeline Hazardous Materials Safety Administration

PHS	Public Health Service
PI	Potential Indicators
PM	Protective Measures
PPE	Personal Protective Equipment
PSA	Protective Security Advisor
PSAP	Public Safety Answering Points
R&D	Research and Development
RCCC	Regional Consortium Coordinating Council
RIAB	Risk Integration and Analysis Branch
RMA	Risk Mitigation Activities
RMWG	Risk Mitigation Working Group
S&T	Science and Technology (DHS Directorate)
SAR	Search and Rescue
SAV	Site Assistance Visit
SCADA	Supervisory Control and Data Acquisition
SCC	Sector Coordinating Council
SERRI	Southeast Region Research Initiative
SIOC	Strategic Information and Operations Center
SLGCP	Office of State and Local Government Coordination and Preparedness
SLTTGCC	State, Local, Tribal and Territorial Government Coordinating Council
SME	Subject Matter Expert
SSA	Sector-Specific Agency
SSP	Sector-Specific Plan
SWAT	Special Weapons And Tactics
UASI	Urban Areas Security Initiative
US&R	Urban Search and Rescue
US-CERT	United States Computer Emergency Readiness Team
USCG	U.S. Coast Guard
USDA	U.S. Department of Agriculture
USFA	U.S. Fire Administration
USFS	U.S. Forest Service
USNORTHCOM	U.S. Northern Command
USPACOM	U.S. Pacific Command
USSS	U.S. Secret Service
UTL	Universal Task List

VA	Department of Veterans Affairs
VBIED	Vehicle-Borne Improvised Explosive Device
WMD	Weapons of Mass Destruction

Appendix 2: Glossary

Many of the definitions in this glossary are derived from language enacted in Federal laws or included in national plans. Sources include the Homeland Security Act of 2002, the USA PATRIOT Act of 2001, the National Infrastructure Protection Plan (NIPP), the National Incident Management System (NIMS), and the National Response Framework (NRF).

All-Hazards Approach. An approach for prevention, protection, preparedness, response, and recovery that addresses a full range of threats and hazards, including domestic terrorist attacks, natural and manmade disasters, accidental disruptions, and other emergencies.

Asset. Contracts, facilities, property, electronic and non-electronic records and documents, unobligated or unexpended balances of appropriations, and other funds or resources (other than personnel).

Awareness. Operational, Situational, Strategic, and Tactical.

- *Operational Awareness.* This is usually defined as close and continuous observation and monitoring of operations in a particular area or sector. The emphasis is on monitoring or surveillance to determine rhythm, salient normal characteristics (including acquiring an understanding of the parameters that define normal behaviors), and indicators and explanations of aberrant behavior. Operational awareness also includes analysis sufficient to determine the importance of deviations, and at least a preliminary understanding of impacts and implications. Operational awareness complements situational awareness.

- *Situational Awareness.* This means paying focused and contextual attention to the surroundings—the overall operating environment. It means taking time before and during an incident (to the extent possible) to take an in-depth look at things and being alert to subtle differences or ongoing changes and interactions. Situational awareness is proactive in nature and intended to identify dangers, implications, and ramifications—in advance, if possible, or very quickly at the time of an incident. Ultimately, the purpose of situational awareness is to avoid surprise and enable an effective response sooner and more successfully. With effective situational awareness, we are more likely to gain control over at least a portion of the event, and our reactions to it may occur earlier than otherwise would be the case. Exercising situational awareness means monitoring and understanding different types of environments and pre-incident indicators so that, for example, contingency plans and increased levels of safety may be implemented as soon as possible.

- *Strategic Awareness.* This is the ability to recognize key factors and the overall context (the "big picture") derived from operational and situational awareness and the need to identify specific goals. Strategic awareness results from evaluating current use, operational behavior in normal and stressed situations, strengths, growth or positive potentials, risks and uncertainties, and known vulnerabilities. This evaluation leads to an awareness of possibilities and needs in a given area or sector that, in turn, nurtures ideas and steps to enhance longer term objectives (e.g., greater protection) for the sector.

- *Tactical Awareness.* This is the ability to see the range of possible near-term steps for accomplishing strategic goals and to evaluate which ones may be best to take. It recognizes that at any given time and in any situation there are often several possible actions that could accomplish those goals, and that there may be resources in the current situation to support these steps.

Business Continuity. The ability of an organization to continue to function before, during, and after a disaster.

Catastrophic Incident. Any natural or manmade incident—including an act of terrorism—that results in extraordinary levels of casualties, damage, or disruption, severely affecting the population, infrastructure, environment, economy, national morale, and/or governmental functions. A catastrophic event could result in sustained national impacts over a prolonged period of time; almost immediately exceeds resources normally available to State, local, tribal, and private sector authorities in the impacted area; and significantly interrupts governmental operations and emergency services so much that national security could be threatened.

Consequence. The result of a terrorist attack or other hazard that reflects the level, duration, and nature of the loss resulting from the incident. For the purposes of the NIPP, consequences are divided into four main categories: public health and safety, economic, psychological, and governance impacts.

Control Systems. Computer-based systems used within many infrastructure and industries to monitor and control sensitive processes and physical functions. These systems typically collect measurement and operational data from the field, process and display the information, and relay control commands to local or remote equipment or human-machine interfaces (operators). Examples of types of control systems include Supervisory Control and Data Acquisition systems, Process Control Systems, and Digital Control Systems.

Critical Infrastructure. Assets, systems, and networks, whether physical or virtual, so vital to the United States that the incapacity or destruction of such assets, systems, or networks would have a debilitating impact on security, national economic security, public health or safety, or any combination of those matters.

Critical Infrastructure and Key Resources (CIKR) Partner. Entities that share in the responsibility for protecting the Nation's CIKR, including Federal, State, regional, local, tribal, or territorial government entities; private sector owners and operators and representative organizations; academic and professional entities; and certain not-for-profit and private volunteer organizations.

Critical Infrastructure Information (CII). Information that is not customarily in the public domain and is related to the security of critical infrastructure or protected systems. CII consists of records and information concerning any of the following:

- Actual, potential, or threatened interference with, attack on, compromise of, or incapacitation of critical infrastructure or protected systems by either physical or computer-based attack or other similar conduct (including the misuse of or unauthorized access to all types of communications and data transmission systems) that violates Federal, State, or local law; harms interstate commerce of the United States; or threatens public health or safety;

- The ability of any critical infrastructure or protected system to resist such interference, compromise, or incapacitation, including any planned or past assessment, projection, or estimate of the vulnerability of critical infrastructure or a protected system, including security testing, risk evaluation thereto, risk management planning, or risk audit; and

- Any planned or past operational problem or solution regarding critical infrastructure or protected systems, including repair, recovery, reconstruction, insurance, or continuity, to the extent it is related to such interference, compromise, or incapacitation.

Critical Infrastructure Partnership Advisory Council (CIPAC). The CIPAC directly supports the sector partnership model by providing a legal framework for members of the Sector Coordinating Councils (SCCs) and Government Coordinating Councils (GCCs) to engage in joint CIKR protection-related activities. The CIPAC serves as a forum for government and private sector partners to engage in a broad spectrum of activities, such as:

- Planning, coordination, implementation, and operational issues;

- Implementation of security programs;

- Operational activities related to CIKR protection, including incident response, recovery, and reconstitution; and

- Development and support of national plans, including the NIPP and the Sector-Specific Plans (SSPs).

- The CIPAC membership consists of private sector CIKR owners and operators, or their representative trade or equivalent associations, from the respective sector's recognized SCC, and representatives of Federal, State, local, and tribal government entities (including their representative trade or equivalent associations) that comprise the corresponding GCC for each sector. DHS published a Federal Register Notice on March 24, 2006, announcing the establishment of CIPAC as a Federal Advisory Committee Act-exempt body, pursuant to section 871 of the Homeland Security Act.

Cybersecurity. The prevention of damage to, unauthorized use of, or exploitation of, and, if needed, the restoration of electronic information and communications systems and the information contained therein to ensure confidentiality, integrity, and availability. Includes protection and restoration, when needed, of information networks and wireline, wireless, satellite, public safety answering points, and 9-1-1 communications systems and control systems.

Emergency Operations Center (EOC). The physical location at which the coordination of information and resources to support domestic incident management activities normally takes place. An EOC may be a temporary facility or may be located in a more central or permanently established facility, perhaps at a higher level of organization within a jurisdiction. EOCs may be organized by major functional disciplines (e.g., fire, law enforcement, medical services), by jurisdiction (e.g., Federal, State, local, tribal), or by some combination.

Emergency Response Provider/Emergency Responders. Includes Federal, State, local, and tribal emergency public safety, law enforcement, emergency response, emergency medical, and related personnel, agencies, and authorities. See section 2(6), Homeland Security Act of 2002, Public Law 107-296, 116 Stat. 2135 (2002).

Emergency Support Function (ESF). FEMA coordinates response support from across the Federal Government and certain nongovernmental organizations (NGOs) by calling up, as needed, one or more of the 15 ESFs. ESFs are coordinated by FEMA through its National Response Coordination Center (NRCC). During a response, ESFs are a critical mechanism to coordinate functional capabilities and resources provided by Federal departments and agencies, along with certain private sector and NGOs. They represent an effective way to bundle and funnel resources and capabilities to State, local, tribal, and other responders. These functions are coordinated by a single agency but may rely on several agencies that provide resources for each functional area. The mission of the ESFs is to provide the greatest possible access to capabilities of the Federal Government regardless of which agency has those capabilities. The ESFs serve as the primary operational-level mechanism to provide assistance in functional areas such as transportation, communications, public works and engineering, firefighting, mass care, housing, human services, public health and medical services, search and rescue, agriculture and natural resources, and energy.

Essential Functions. Essential Emergency Services Sector (ESS) functions involve people, property, facilities, information, equipment, and systems, or any combination, that focus on protecting communities on a daily basis, saving lives, and preventing further property damage in a disaster or other emergency. Essential functions for the ESS also include actions taken by these specially trained and organized elements to return their communities to normal, or even safer, situations following emergencies.

Federal Coordinating Officer (FCO). For Stafford Act incidents (i.e., emergencies or major disasters), on the recommendation of the FEMA Administrator and the Secretary of Homeland Security, the President appoints an FCO. The FCO is a senior FEMA official trained, certified, and well experienced in emergency management, and specifically appointed to coordinate Federal support in the response to and recovery from emergencies and major disasters. The FCO executes Stafford Act authorities, including commitment of FEMA resources and the mission assignment of other Federal departments or agencies. If a major disaster or emergency declaration covers a geographic area that spans all or parts of more than one State, the President may decide to appoint a single FCO for the entire incident, with other individuals as needed serving as Deputy FCOs.

In all cases, the FCO represents the FEMA Administrator in the field to discharge all FEMA responsibilities for the response and recovery efforts underway. For Stafford Act events, the FCO is the primary Federal representative with whom the State Coordinating Officer and other State, tribal, and local response officials interface to determine the most urgent needs and set objectives for an effective response in collaboration with the Unified Coordination Group.

Federal Departments and Agencies. The term "Federal departments and agencies" means those executive departments enumerated in 5 United States Code (U.S.C.) 101, together with the DHS; independent establishments as defined by 5 U.S.C. 104(1); government corporations as defined by 5 U.S.C. 103(1); and the United States Postal Service.

First Responder. Designation for a person who, in the course of their professional duties of responding to emergencies and in the early stages of an incident, is responsible for the protection and preservation of life, property, evidence, the environment, and for meeting basic human needs. *(Emergency Responder is used interchangeably with First Responder)* Reference: Homeland Security Act of 2002 – Section 2, Paragraph (6); Public Law 107-296; U.S.C. 101(6); National Response Framework.

Function. In the context of the NIPP, function is defined as the service, process, capability, or operation performed by specific infrastructure assets, systems, and networks.

Government Coordinating Council. The government counterpart to the SCC for each sector established to enable inter-agency coordination. The GCC is comprised of representatives across various levels of government (Federal, State, local, tribal, and territorial) as appropriate to the security and operational landscape of each individual sector.

Hazard. Something that is potentially dangerous or harmful, often the root cause of an unwanted outcome.

Homeland Infrastructure Threat and Risk Analysis Center (HITRAC). DHS HITRAC conducts integrated threat and risk analyses for CIKR sectors. HITRAC is a joint fusion center that spans both the Office of Intelligence and Analysis (I&A)—a member of the Intelligence Community—and the Office of Infrastructure Protection (IP). As called for in section 201 of the Homeland Security Act, HITRAC brings together intelligence and infrastructure specialists to ensure a sufficient understanding of the risks to the Nation's CIKR from foreign and domestic threats. HITRAC works in partnership with the U.S. Intelligence Community and national law enforcement to integrate and analyze intelligence and law enforcement information in threat and risk analysis products. HITRAC also works in partnership with the Sector-Specific Agencies (SSAs) and owners and operators to ensure that their expertise on infrastructure operations is integrated into HITRAC's analysis. HITRAC develops analytical products by combining threat assessments based on all source information and intelligence analysis with vulnerability and consequence assessments. This process provides an understanding of the threat, CIKR vulnerabilities, and potential consequences of attacks. When identified, the analyses also include potential options for managing the risk. This combination of intelligence and practical CIKR knowledge allows DHS to provide products that contain strategically relevant and actionable information. It also allows DHS to identify intelligence collection requirements in conjunction with CIKR partners so that the intelligence community can provide the type of information necessary to support the CIKR risk management and protection missions. HITRAC coordinates closely with partners outside the Federal Government through the SCCs, GCCs, Information Sharing and Analysis Centers (ISACs), and State and Local Fusion Centers to ensure that its products are accessible and relevant to partner needs.

Homeland Security Information Network (HSIN). HSIN is a national, Web-based communications platform that allows DHS; SSAs; State, local, tribal, and territorial government entities; and other partners to obtain, analyze, and share information based on a common operating picture of strategic risk and the evolving incident landscape. The network is designed to provide a robust, dynamic information-sharing capability that supports both NIPP-related steady-state CIKR protection and National Response Framework (NRF)-related incident management activities, and to provide the information-sharing processes that form the bridge between these two homeland security missions. HSIN is one part of the Information-Sharing Environment (ISE) called for by the Intelligence Reform and Terrorism Prevention Act of 2004; as specified in the act, it will provide users with access to terrorism information that is matched to their roles, responsibilities, and missions in a timely and responsive manner.

Incident. An occurrence or event, natural or manmade, that requires an emergency response to protect life or property. Examples of incidents can include major disasters, emergencies, terrorist attacks, terrorist threats, wildland and urban fires, floods, hazardous materials spills, nuclear accidents, aircraft accidents, earthquakes, hurricanes, tornadoes, tropical storms, war-related disasters, public health and medical emergencies, and other occurrences requiring an emergency response.

Incident Command System (ICS). Much of NIMS is built on ICS, which was developed by the Federal, State, and local wildland fire agencies during the 1970s. ICS is normally structured to facilitate activities in five major functional areas: command, operations, planning, logistics, and finance/administration. In some circumstances, intelligence and investigations may be added as a sixth functional area.

Information Sharing and Analysis Centers. Underscoring effective cybersecurity efforts is the importance of information sharing between and among industry and government. To this end, the Information Technology and Communications ISACs work closely together and with DHS and the SSAs to maximize resources, coordinate preparedness and response efforts, and maintain situational awareness to enable risk mitigation regarding cyber infrastructure.

Infrastructure. The framework of interdependent networks and systems comprising identifiable industries, institutions (including people and procedures), and distribution capabilities that provide a reliable flow of products and services essential to the defense and economic security of the United States, the smooth functioning of government at all levels, and society as a whole. Consistent with the definition in the Homeland Security Act, infrastructure includes physical, cyber, and human elements.

Interdependency. The multi- or bi-directional reliance of an asset, system, network, or collection thereof, within or across sectors, on input, interaction, or other requirement from other sources in order to function properly.

Joint Field Office (JFO). The JFO is the primary Federal incident management field structure. The JFO is a temporary Federal facility that provides a central location for the coordination of Federal, State, local, and tribal governments and private sector organizations and NGOs with primary responsibility for response and recovery. The JFO structure is organized, staffed, and managed in a manner consistent with NIMS principles and is led by the Unified Coordination Group. Although the JFO uses an ICS structure, the JFO does not manage on-scene operations. Instead, the JFO focuses on providing support to on-scene efforts and conducting broader support operations that may extend beyond the incident site.

Joint Information Center (JIC). The JIC is responsible for the coordination and dissemination of information for the public and media concerning an incident. JICs may be established locally, regionally, or nationally depending on the size and magnitude of the incident.

Joint Operations Center (JOC). The JOC is an inter-agency command post established by the FBI to manage terrorist threats or incidents and investigative and intelligence activities. The JOC coordinates the necessary Federal, State, and local assets required to support the investigation, and to prepare for, respond to, and resolve the threat or incident.

Jurisdiction. A range or sphere of authority. Public agencies have jurisdiction at an incident related to their legal responsibilities and authority. Jurisdictional authority at an incident can be political or geographical (e.g., according to Federal, State, city, county, tribal, or territorial boundaries), or functional (e.g., law enforcement, public health).

Key Resources. As defined in the Homeland Security Act, key resources are publicly or privately controlled resources essential to the minimal operations of the economy and government.

Local Government. Local government includes any county, municipality, city, town, township, local public authority, school district, special district, intrastate district, council of governments (regardless of whether the council is incorporated as a nonprofit corporation under State law), regional or interstate government entity, or agency or instrumentality of a local government; an Indian tribe, authorized tribal organization, or (in Alaska) a native village or Alaska Regional Native Corporation; and a rural community, unincorporated town or village, or other public entity.

Major Disasters and Emergencies. Major disasters, as defined by the Stafford Act, are any natural catastrophe (including any hurricane, tornado, storm, high water, wind-driven water, tidal wave, tsunami, earthquake, volcanic eruption, landslide, mudslide, snowstorm, or drought) or, regardless of cause, any fire, flood, or explosion, in any part of the United States, which in the determination of the President causes damage of sufficient severity and magnitude to warrant major disaster assistance under the Stafford Act to supplement the efforts and available resources of States, local governments, and disaster relief organizations in alleviating the damage, loss, hardship, or suffering caused thereby. Emergencies, as defined by the Stafford Act, are any other occasion or instance for which, in the determination of the President, Federal assistance is needed to supplement State and local efforts and capabilities to save lives and to protect property and public health and safety, or to lessen or avert the threat of a catastrophe in any part of the United States.

Mitigation. Activities designed to reduce or eliminate risks to persons or property or to lessen the actual or potential effects or consequences of an incident. Mitigation measures may be implemented prior to, during, or after an incident. Mitigation measures are often developed in accordance with lessons learned from prior incidents. Mitigation involves ongoing actions to reduce exposure to, probability of, or potential loss from hazards. Measures may include zoning and building codes, floodplain buyouts, and analysis of hazard-related data to determine where it is safe to build or locate temporary facilities. Mitigation can include efforts to educate governments, businesses, and the public on measures they can take to reduce loss and injury.

Mutual Aid Agreement (MAA). Executing mutual aid and other agreements established prior to an incident with appropriate entities at the local, tribal, State, and Federal levels is an important element of preparedness, along with the readiness to develop/implement new agreements during the life cycle of an incident.

National Communications System (NCS). The mission of the NCS is to assist the President, National Security Council, Director of the Office of Science and Technology Policy (OSTP), and Director of the Office of Management and Budget (OMB) in: (1) the exercise of the telecommunications functions and responsibilities; and (2) coordination of the planning for and provision of national security and emergency preparedness communications for the Federal Government under all circumstances, including crisis or emergency, attack, and recovery and reconstitution.

The NCS also participates in joint industry-government planning through its work with the President's National Security Telecommunications Advisory Committee, through the NCS's National Coordinating Center for Telecommunications (NCC), and the NCC's subordinate Communications ISAC.

National Coordinating Center for Telecommunications. Pursuant to Executive Order 12472, the National Communications System (NCS) assists the President, National Security Council, Homeland Security Council, OSTP, and OMB in the coordination and provision of National Security and Emergency Preparedness (NS/EP) communications for the Federal Government under all circumstances, including crisis or emergency, attack, recovery, and reconstitution. As called for in the Executive order, the NCS has established the NCC, which is a joint industry-government entity. Under the Executive Order, the NCC assists the NCS in the initiation, coordination, restoration, and reconstitution of national security or emergency preparedness communications services or facilities under all conditions of crisis or emergency. The NCC regularly monitors the status of communications systems. It collects situational and operational information on a regular basis, as well as during a crisis, and provides information to the NCS. The NCS, in turn, shares information with the White House and other DHS components.

National Counter Terrorism Center (NCTC). The NCTC serves as the primary Federal organization for integrating and analyzing all intelligence pertaining to terrorism and counterterrorism and for conducting strategic operational planning by integrating all instruments of national power.

National Incident Management System. NIMS is a system mandated by Homeland Security Presidential Directive 5 (HSPD-5) that provides a consistent, nationwide approach for Federal, State, local, and tribal governments; the private sector; and NGOs to work together effectively and efficiently to prepare for, respond to, and recover from domestic incidents, regardless of cause, size, or complexity. To provide for compatibility and interoperability among Federal, State, local, and tribal capabilities, NIMS uses a core set of concepts, principles, and terminology. HSPD-5 identifies these as the ICS; multiagency coordination systems;

training; identification and management of resources (including systems for classifying types of resources); qualification and certification; and the collection, tracking, and reporting of incident information and incident resources.

National Infrastructure Coordinating Center (NICC). The NICC monitors the Nation's critical infrastructure and key resources on an ongoing basis. During an incident, the NICC provides a coordinating forum to share information across critical infrastructure and key resources sectors through appropriate information-sharing entities such as the ISACs and SCCs.

National Operations Center (NOC). Serves as the national fusion center, collecting and synthesizing all-source information, including information from State fusion centers, across all threats and all hazards, covering the spectrum of homeland security partners. Federal departments and agencies should report information regarding actual or potential incidents requiring a coordinated Federal response to the NOC. NOC operational components are the NRCC and NICC.

National Response Coordination Center. The NRCC is FEMA's primary operations management center, as well as the focal point for national resource coordination. As a 24/7 operations center, the NRCC monitors potential or developing incidents and supports the efforts of regional and field components. The NRCC also has the capacity to increase staffing immediately in anticipation of or in response to an incident by activating the full range of Emergency Support Functions and other personnel as needed to provide resources and policy guidance to a JFO or other local incident management structures. The NRCC provides overall emergency management coordination, conducts operational planning, deploys national-level entities, and collects and disseminates incident information as it builds and maintains a common operating picture. Representatives of nonprofit organizations within the private sector may participate in the NRCC to enhance information exchange and cooperation between these entities and the Federal Government.

National Response Framework. NRF is a guide to how the Nation conducts all-hazards response. It is built on scalable, flexible, and adaptable coordinating structures to align key roles and responsibilities across the Nation, linking all levels of government, NGOs, and the private sector. It is intended to capture specific authorities and best practices for managing incidents that range from the serious but purely local, to large-scale terrorist attacks or catastrophic natural disasters.

National Special Security Event. Any event that, by virtue of its political, economic, social, or religious significance, may be the target of terrorism or other criminal activity.

Network. In the context of the NIPP, a network is a group of assets or systems that share information or interact with each other to provide infrastructure services within or across sectors.

Nongovernmental Organization. NGOs are based on the interests of their members. They are not created by a government, but may work cooperatively with government. Such organizations serve a public purpose, not a private one. Examples of NGOs are faith-based charity organizations and the American Red Cross.

Normalize. In the context of the NIPP, the process of transforming risk-related data into comparable units.

Owners and Operators. Those entities responsible for day-to-day operation and investment in a particular asset or system.

Partnership for Critical Infrastructure Security (PCIS). The PCIS membership is comprised of one or more members and their alternates from each of the SCCs. The partnership coordinates cross-sector initiatives to support CIKR protection by identifying legislative issues that affect such initiatives and by raising awareness of issues in CIKR protection. The primary activities of the PCIS include:

- Providing senior-level, cross-sector strategic coordination through partnership with DHS and the SSAs;

- Identifying and disseminating CIKR protection best practices across the sectors;

- Participating in coordinated planning efforts related to the development, implementation, and revision of the NIPP and SSPs; and

- Coordinating with DHS to support efforts to plan and execute the Nation's CIKR protection mission.

Preparedness. The range of deliberate critical tasks and activities necessary to build, sustain, and improve the operational capability to prevent, protect against, respond to, and recover from domestic incidents. Preparedness is a continuous process involving efforts at all levels of government and between government and private sector and NGOs to identify threats, determine vulnerabilities, and identify required activities and resources to mitigate risk.

Prevention. Actions taken to avoid an incident or to intervene to stop an incident from occurring. Prevention involves actions taken to protect lives and property. It involves applying intelligence and other information to a range of activities that may include such countermeasures as deterrence operations; heightened inspections; improved surveillance and security operations; investigations to determine the full nature and source of the threat; immunizations, isolation, or quarantine; public health and agricultural surveillance and testing processes; and, as appropriate, specific law enforcement operations aimed at deterring, preempting, interdicting, or disrupting illegal activity and apprehending potential perpetrators and bringing them to justice.

Primary Attack. Deliberate violence directed at humans or infrastructure with the intent to maim, injure, kill, damage, or destroy, and to undermine national security, prestige, morale, and economic prosperity.

Principal Federal Official (PFO). By law and by Presidential directive, the Secretary of Homeland Security is the principal Federal official responsible for coordination of all domestic incidents requiring multiagency Federal response. The Secretary may elect to designate a single individual to serve as his or her primary representative to ensure consistency of Federal support as well as the overall effectiveness of the Federal incident management. When appointed, such an individual serves in the field as the PFO for the incident. Congress has provided that, notwithstanding the general prohibition on appointing a PFO for Stafford Act incidents, "there may be instances in which FEMA should not be the lead agency in charge of the response, such as a pandemic outbreak or an Olympic event." In such cases, the Secretary may assign a PFO. Congress also recognized that there may be "major non-Stafford Act responses that may include a Stafford Act component." In such cases, also, the Secretary may assign a PFO. The Secretary will only appoint a PFO for catastrophic or unusually complex incidents that require extraordinary coordination. When appointed, the PFO interfaces with Federal, State, local, and tribal jurisdictional officials regarding the overall Federal incident management strategy and acts as the primary Federal spokesperson for coordinated media and public communications. The PFO serves as a member of the Unified Coordination Group and provides a primary point of contact and situational awareness locally for the Secretary of Homeland Security. A PFO is a senior Federal official with proven management experience and strong leadership capabilities. The PFO deploys with a small, highly trained mobile support staff. Both the PFO and support staff undergo specific training prior to appointment to their respective positions. Once formally designated for an ongoing incident, a PFO relinquishes the conduct of all previous duties to focus exclusively on his or her incident management responsibilities. The same individual will not serve as the PFO and the FCO (see below) at the same time for the same incident. When both positions are assigned, the FCO will have responsibility for administering Stafford Act authorities, as described below. The Secretary is not restricted to DHS officials when selecting a PFO.

The PFO does not direct or replace the incident command structure established at the incident. Nor does the PFO have directive authority over a FCO, a Senior Federal Law Enforcement Official, a DoD Joint Task Force Commander, or any other Federal or State official. Other Federal incident management officials retain their authorities as defined in existing statutes and directives. Rather, the PFO promotes collaboration and, as possible, resolves any Federal inter-agency conflict that may arise. The PFO identifies and presents to the Secretary of Homeland Security any policy issues that require resolution.

Prioritization. In the context of the NIPP, prioritization is the process of using risk assessment results to identify where risk reduction or mitigation efforts are most needed and subsequently determine which protective actions should be instituted in order to have the greatest effect.

Private Sector. The private sector consists of organizations and entities that are not part of any governmental structure. This includes for-profit and not-for-profit organizations, formal and informal structures, commerce and industry, private emergency response organizations, and private voluntary organizations. Because private industry owns and operates the vast majority of the Nation's CIKR, its involvement is crucial for implementation of the NIPP. Private sector owners and operators remain the first line of defense for their own facilities; they routinely carry out risk management planning and invest in protective measures as a necessary business function. Through various means, the private sector obtains and shares security information with Federal, State, local, and tribal agencies. The DHS has established the Protected Critical Infrastructure Information (PCII) Program to enable the private sector to voluntarily submit infrastructure information to the Federal Government without compromising data security.

Protect and Secure. The expression "protect and secure," as defined in HSPD-7, means reducing the vulnerability of CIKR in order to deter, neutralize, or mitigate terrorist attacks. Thus, as described in this SSP, critical infrastructure protection includes the activities that identify CIKR, assess vulnerabilities, prioritize CIKR, and develop protective programs and measures, because these activities ultimately lead to implementation of protective strategies to reduce vulnerability.

Protected Critical Infrastructure Information. PCII refers to all critical infrastructure information, including categorical inclusion PCII, that has undergone the validation process and that the PCII Program Office has determined qualifies for protection under the CII Act. All information submitted to the PCII Program Office or Designee with an express statement is presumed to be PCII until the PCII Program Office determines otherwise.

Protection. Actions to mitigate the overall risk to CIKR assets, systems, networks, or their interconnecting links resulting from exposure, injury, destruction, incapacitation, or exploitation. In the context of the NIPP, protection includes actions to deter the threat, mitigate vulnerabilities, or minimize consequences associated with a terrorist attack or other incident. Protection can include a wide range of activities, such as hardening facilities, building resiliency and redundancy, incorporating hazard resistance into initial facility design, initiating active or passive countermeasures, installing security systems, promoting workforce surety, and implementing cybersecurity measures, among various others.

Protective Security Advisor (PSA) Program. DHS CIKR protection and vulnerability assessment specialists are assigned as liaisons between DHS and the protective community at the State, local, and private sector levels in geographical areas representing major concentrations of CIKR across the United States. PSAs are responsible for sharing risk information and providing technical assistance to local law enforcement and owners and operators of CIKR within their respective areas of responsibility.

Public Information Officer. A member of the PFO command staff responsible for interfacing with the public and media or with other agencies with incident-related information requirements.

Recovery. The development, coordination, and execution of service- and site-restoration plans for impacted communities and the reconstitution of government operations and services through individual, private sector, nongovernmental, and public assistance programs that identify needs and define resources; provide housing and promote restoration; address long-term care and treatment of affected persons; implement additional measures for community restoration; incorporate mitigation measures and techniques, as feasible; evaluate the incident to identify lessons learned; and develop initiatives to mitigate the effects of future incidents.

Resilience. In the context of the NIPP, resilience is the capability of an asset, system, or network to maintain its function during or to recover from a terrorist attack or other incident.

Response. Activities that address the short-term, direct effects of an incident, including immediate actions to save lives, protect property, and meet basic human needs.

Response also includes the execution of emergency operations plans and incident mitigation activities designed to limit the loss of life, personal injury, property damage, and other unfavorable outcomes. As indicated by the situation, response activities include applying intelligence and other information to lessen the effects or consequences of an incident; increased security operations; continuing investigations into the nature and source of the threat; ongoing surveillance and testing processes; immunizations, isolation, or quarantine; and specific law enforcement operations aimed at preempting, interdicting, or disrupting illegal activity, and apprehending actual perpetrators and bringing them to justice.

Risk. A measure of potential harm that encompasses threat, vulnerability, and consequence. In the context of the NIPP, risk is the expected magnitude of loss due to a terrorist attack, natural disaster, or other incident, along with the likelihood of such an event occurring and causing that loss.

Risk Management Framework. A planning methodology that outlines the process for setting goals; identifying assets, systems, networks, and functions; assessing risks; prioritizing and implementing protective programs; measuring performance; and taking corrective action. Public and private sector entities often include risk management frameworks in their business continuity plans.

Secondary Attack. An assault following a primary attack meant to injure, maim, or kill first responders or other bystanders as they attempt to aid victims and secure the site of the primary attack.

Sector. A logical collection of assets, systems, or networks that provide a common function to the economy, government, or society. The NIPP addresses 18 CIKR sectors, as identified by the criteria set forth in HSPD-7.

Sector Coordinating Council. The private sector counterpart to the GCCs, these councils are self-organized, self-run, and self-governed organizations that are representative of a spectrum of key stakeholders within a sector. SCCs serve as the government's principal point of entry into each sector for developing and coordinating a wide range of CIKR protection activities and issues.

Sector Partnership Model. The framework used to promote and facilitate sector and cross-sector planning, coordination, collaboration, and information sharing for CIKR protection involving all levels of government and private sector entities.

Sector-Specific Agency. Federal departments and agencies identified in HSPD-7 as responsible for CIKR protection activities in specified CIKR sectors.

Sector-Specific Plan. Augmenting plans that complement and extend the NIPP Base Plan and detail the application of the NIPP framework specific to each CIKR sector. SSPs are developed by the SSAs in close collaboration with other sector partners.

State. Refers to any State of the United States, the District of Columbia, Commonwealth of Puerto Rico, U.S. Virgin Islands, Guam, American Samoa, Commonwealth of the Northern Mariana Islands, the Freely Associated States (i.e., Republic of Palau, Federated States of Micronesia, and Republic of the Marshall Islands), and any possession of the United States.

State Homeland Security Advisors (HSAs). The HSA serves as counsel to the Governor on homeland security issues and may serve as a liaison between the Governor's office, the State homeland security structure, DHS, and other organizations both inside and outside of the State. The advisor often chairs a committee comprised of representatives of relevant State agencies, including public safety, the National Guard, emergency management, public health, and others charged with developing prevention, protection, response, and recovery strategies. This also includes preparedness activities associated with these strategies.

Steady State. In the context of the NIPP, steady state is the posture for routine, normal, day to-day operations as contrasted with temporary periods of heightened alert or real-time response to threats or incidents.

Strategic Information and Operations Center (SIOC). The FBI SIOC is the focal point and operational control center for all Federal intelligence, law enforcement, and investigative law enforcement activities related to domestic terrorist incidents or credible threats, including leading attribution investigations. The SIOC serves as an information clearinghouse to help collect, process, vet, and disseminate, in a timely manner, information relevant to law enforcement and criminal investigation efforts. The SIOC maintains direct connectivity with the NOC. The SIOC, located at FBI Headquarters, supports the FBI's mission in leading efforts of the law enforcement community to detect, prevent, preempt, and disrupt terrorist attacks against the United States.

Subject Matter Expert (SME). A technical expert in a specific area or in performing a specialized job or task.

System. In the context of the NIPP, a system is a collection of assets, resources, or elements that performs a process that provides infrastructure services to the Nation.

Terrorism. Any activity that: (1) involves an act that is (a) dangerous to human life or potentially destructive of critical infrastructure or key resources, and (b) a violation of the criminal laws of the United States or of any State or other subdivision of the United States; and (2) appears to be intended to (a) intimidate or coerce a civilian population, (b) influence the policy of a government by intimidation or coercion, or (c) affect the conduct of a government by mass destruction, assassination, or kidnapping.

Threat. In the context of the NIPP, threat means the intention and capability of an adversary to undertake actions that would be detrimental to CIKR.

United States Computer Emergency Readiness Team (US-CERT). DHS established the US-CERT, which is a 24/7 single point of contact for cyberspace analysis and warning, information sharing, and incident response and recovery for a broad range of users, including government, enterprises, small businesses, and home users. US-CERT is a partnership between DHS and the public and private sectors designed to help secure the Nation's Internet infrastructure and to coordinate defenses against and responses to cyber attacks across the Nation. US-CERT is responsible for:

- Analyzing and reducing cyber threats and vulnerabilities;
- Disseminating cyber threat warning information; and
- Coordinating cyber incident response activities.

Value Proposition. A statement that outlines the national and homeland security interest in protecting the Nation's CIKR and articulates benefits gained by all CIKR partners through the risk management framework and public-private partnership described in the NIPP.

Vulnerability. A weakness in the design, implementation, or operation of an asset, system, or network that can be exploited by an adversary or disrupted by a natural hazard or technological failure.

Weapons of Mass Destruction. (1) Any explosive, incendiary, or poison gas (i) bomb, (ii) grenade, (iii) rocket having a propellant charge of more than 4 ounces, (iv) missile having an explosive or incendiary charge of more than one-quarter ounce, or (v) mine or (vi) similar device; (2) any weapon that is designed or intended to cause death or serious bodily injury through the release, dissemination, or impact of toxic or poisonous chemicals or their precursors; (3) any weapon involving a disease organism; or (4) any weapon that is designed to release radiation or radioactivity at a level dangerous to human life (18 U.S.C. 2332a).

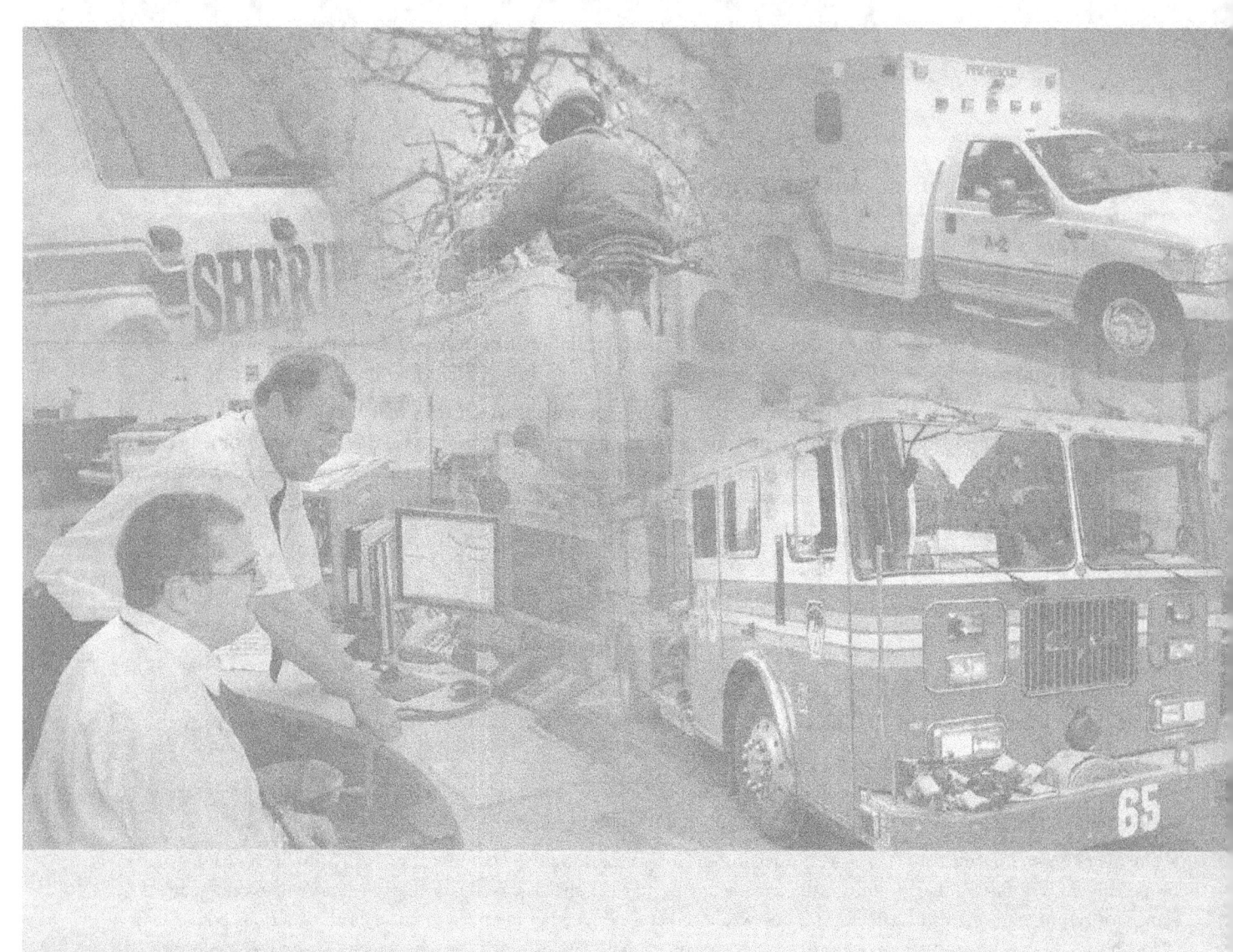

Appendix 3: Protective Programs

Federal, State, Local, and Tribal Protective Programs

Federal, State, local, and tribal governments have sponsored various protective programs that complement and assist the ESS. These include vulnerability and risk assessment processes and methodologies such as Site Assistance Visits (SAVs) and Buffer Zone Plans (BZPs). Additional programs include:

- **Protective Security Advisor (PSA) Program.** PSAs serve as on-site critical infrastructure and vulnerability assessment specialists for DHS and are assigned to 70 districts in 50 States and one territory. PSAs are a link between State, local, tribal, territorial, and private sector organizations and DHS infrastructure protection resources.

The PSA's primary responsibilities are to:

  - Assist with ongoing State and local CIKR security efforts by interacting with State Homeland Security Advisors and other State, local, tribal, territorial and private sector organizations;

  - Support the development of the national risk picture by identifying, assessing, monitoring, and minimizing risk to critical assets at the local and regional levels;

  - Serve as communication conduits for officials and private sector owners and operators of CIKR assets seeking to communicate with DHS;

  - Coordinate vulnerability assessments, training, grants, and other forms of technical assistance;

  - Serve as the on-scene Office of Infrastructure Protection (IP) representative within State and local Emergency Operations Centers (EOCs) and as Infrastructure Liaisons at Joint Field Offices (JFOs) as needed during incident response; and

  - Support special event planning and exercises in their district by providing local knowledge of CIKR.

- **Common Vulnerabilities (CV), Potential Indicators (PI), and Protective Measures (PM) Reports.** Based on data gathered from SAVs and Buffer Zone Plans, DHS has developed three types of reports for local law enforcement and asset owners and operators to help them better secure CIKR assets. CVs identify common characteristics and vulnerabilities at specific types of CIKR assets. PIs provide information on how to detect terrorist activity in areas surrounding CIKR assets. PMs identify best practices and other protective measures for use at specific types of CIKR assets and systems. These reports have been distributed to all State homeland security offices with guidance to share these reports with the owners and operators of critical infrastructure, the law enforcement community within each State, and Captains of the Port.

- **Bombing Prevention.** DHS's Office for Bombing Prevention (OBP) is actively engaged in congressionally mandated protective programs designed to improve national bombing prevention preparedness at all levels of government, among the public, and within the private sector. OBP directly supports the Homeland Security Council's (HSC) National Improvised

Explosive Device Task Force and leads the DHS IED Working Group (IEDWG) in its mandate to coordinate national and inter-governmental bombing prevention activities.

Selected protective programs that benefit the ESS include:

- **Improvised Explosive Device (IED)** Awareness workshops provide State, local, and tribal leaders with improved knowledge of current IED threats and insight into resource and planning considerations;

- **The Bomb-Making Materials Awareness Program** provides State, local, and tribal law enforcement with information on consumer materials that could be used to create homemade explosives or other IEDs. The program is designed to forge the awareness relationship between patrol officers and point-of-sale employees, and to enhance private sector security at no incremental cost;

- **TRIPwire** provides technical and operational information on terrorist tactics, techniques, and procedures (TTPs) to the desktop of decision makers and officers in the bombing prevention community; and

- **Multi-Jurisdiction Bombing Prevention Plans** provide a consistent and repeatable planning process to help high-risk urban areas and other vital locations develop thorough bombing prevention and response plans that efficiently integrate assets and capabilities from multiple jurisdictions and the ESS to ensure effective response.

- **Lessons Learned Information-Sharing Web Site.** This site is the national network of lessons learned and best practices for emergency response providers and homeland security officials. Its secure, restricted-access information is designed to facilitate prevention and response to acts of terrorism across all disciplines and communities throughout the United States. **www.llis.dhs.gov**

- **InfraGard.** The FBI InfraGard program is an association of businesses; academic institutions; State, local, and tribal law enforcement agencies; and other participants dedicated to sharing information and intelligence to prevent hostile acts against the United States. The relationship supports information sharing at the national and local levels, and its objectives are to:

  - Increase the level of information and reporting between InfraGard members and the FBI on matters related to counterterrorism, cybercrime, and other major crime programs;

  - Increase interaction and information sharing among InfraGard members and the FBI regarding threats to critical infrastructure, vulnerabilities, and interdependencies;

  - Provide members with value-added threat advisories, alerts, and warnings;

  - Promote effective liaison with Federal, State, and local agencies, including DHS; and

  - Provide members with a forum for education and training on counterterrorism, counterintelligence, cyber crime, and other matters relevant to informed reporting of potential crimes and attacks.

- **State of Colorado's Terrorism Protection Resource Guides.** These guides, published by the State's Office of Preparedness and Security, Homeland Security Section, provide an overview of terrorist objectives, examples of specific threat categories, information on protective measures and their implementation, and a protective measures matrix. The guides are intended to give information that can help determine areas within a facility that are vulnerable to terrorist attack and ways to protect them.

- **National Institute for Occupational Safety and Health National Personal Protective Technology Laboratory.** The laboratory has developed the Personal Protective Equipment (PPE) News Distribution List, an electronic service that automatically sends relevant information to subscribers.

- **Emergency Management Institute (EMI).** The institute provides a diverse listing of more than 50 online correspondence courses (e.g., home protection, terrorism awareness, Incident Command System (ICS)).

- **Commercial Equipment Direct Assistance Program (CEDAP).** The program offers equipment and equipment training in the following categories: detection and sensor devices, law enforcement information-sharing software, risk assessment software, communications interoperability systems, and PPE.

- **Domestic Preparedness Equipment Technical Assistance Program.** This is a comprehensive, national technical assistance program for emergency responders. It provides on-site technical assistance and training to assist emergency responders to better choose, operate, and maintain their Chemical, Biological, Radiological, Nuclear, and Explosives (CBRNE) detection and response equipment.

- **Security Guard Training.** Twenty-two States currently require basic training courses for licensed contract guards. Of these, few specifically require counterterrorism training. In New York City, the police department has developed a public-private partnership called NYPD Shield. This program aims to provide best practices and counterterrorism training opportunities by partnering police officers with private sector security managers.

- **Private Asset and Logistics Management System (PALMS).** This registry of private sector resources was created by the New York Office of Emergency Management. Through PALMS, businesses list goods and services they have available for use by New York City in an emergency. Assets likely needed during emergencies include personnel (e.g., vehicle operators with commercial licenses, personnel with language skills), equipment and supplies (e.g., refrigerated trucks, portable generators, fuel), and facilities (e.g., auditorium space, phone bank capacity). New York City's response agencies will call on PALMS participants to supply assets listed in the registry if the need arises.

- **Emergency Services Relevant Portals. TRIPwire** is a secure, Web-based portal that provides law enforcement and other selected ES partners with unclassified information about terrorist tactics, techniques, and procedures related to IEDs. Currently, only SCC and PCIS leaders, directors of security, and security instructors are eligible to access TRIPwire. A dedicated private sector portal has been developed to deliver sector-specific IED information and protective measures to all private sector partners.

- **Surveillance Detection Training.** The course provides information necessary to develop the knowledge and skills required to establish surveillance detection operations to protect CIKR during elevated threat periods. In addition to providing awareness-level training of terrorist tactics and attack history, the course allows participants to practice the methods of detection and surveillance through practical exercises.

- **IED Awareness Training.** OBP developed a course designed to educate the chemical facilities and supply chain professionals about the threat of IEDs. The course consists of online sessions that provide a basic introduction to the various types of IEDs. In addition, the course outlines how these weapons are used, the components required to build an IED, general hazards and safety precautions associated with IEDs, general search guidelines for bomb threats and suspicious packages, and guidelines to follow in the event of an explosion or bombing incident.

- **Intra-State Mutual Aid System (IMAS).** IMAS provides a national fire service intrastate mutual aid system, which allows the fire service to activate and deploy resources rapidly during a disaster. The program is a partnership between the International Association of Fire Chiefs (IAFC) and the FEMA National Incident Management System Integration Center (NIC).

- **Emergency Management Committee (EMC) Mutual Aid System Task Force (MASTF).** MASTF was established after Hurricane Katrina to help provide better coordination of fire and emergency service response capabilities for disasters and events. Tasks include contributing to national guidance on incident command and credentialing and developing interstate mutual aid plans. The program is a partnership between the IAFC and the NIC. The program also includes the National Mutual Aid Consortium, a cross-disciplinary consortium of fire-based and other emergency services dedicated to mutual aid.

- **National Fire Fighter Near-Miss Reporting System.** This Web-based system collects and analyzes information on near-miss events in order to understand and prevent the issues and environments that lead to responder injury and death. The program was generously implemented with grants from DHS and the Fireman's Fund Insurance Company and is a partnership between the IAFC and the International Association of Fire Fighters (IAFF), as well as 15 additional partners representing fire and emergency service personnel and fire service-related private industry.

- **Wildland Fire Training.** The IAFC partners with the U.S. Department of Agriculture (USDA) Forest Service and the U.S. Department of Interior on education and training initiatives that assist emergency responders to train and prepare their communities for the threats of wildland fire. It also facilitates coordination with Federal and State CIKR partners, particularly in the Wildland Urban Interface (WUI). This work often also includes working collaboratively with other Federal agencies and national level associations.

- **Firefighter Health and Safety.** In conjunction with other fire and emergency services agencies, the IAFC manages a variety of programs that contribute directly to firefighter health and safety. Examples of such programs include the annual Health, Safety and Survival Week (with IAFF), a Wellness-Fitness Initiative (with IAFF, the National Volunteer Fire Council (NVFC), and DHS/USFA), a Sleep Deprivation Study (with DHS/USFA, Oregon Health and Science University), and a variety of vehicle and road safety initiatives (with DHS, U.S. Fire Administration, U.S. Department of Transportation, and responder and private sector associations).

- **IAFC Resource: Model Procedures for Responding to Package with Suspicion of Biological Threat.** The IAFC, in coordination with the FBI Hazardous Materials Response Unit: FBI Laboratory Division, created these model procedures for responding to suspicious packages. **www.iafc.org/downloads** (see under Homeland Security/Terrorism/National Response).

- **IAFC Resource: Terrorism Response: A Checklist and Guide for Fire Chiefs.** The IAFC created this tool to help fire chiefs from departments of all sizes revitalize and refocus their efforts to prepare for, respond to, and recover from acts of terrorism. A second edition was recently released. **www.iafc.org/displaycommon.cfm?an=1&subarticlenbr=807**

Sector Protective Programs

There are many security, safety, and operational guides that could be shared more broadly across the ESS. Sector partners also employ a wide range of protective programs, for their individual facilities and to support their particular functions, which comprise a comprehensive set of best practices that should be considered for ESS applicability. Examples of publications and protective programs follow:

- **IAFF Online Learning Tool.** The tool Influenza Pandemic: What First-Responders Need to Know about Avian Flu assists firefighters and paramedics in preparing for a flu outbreak.

- **IAFC National Fire Service Intrastate Mutual-Aid System.** This project supports creation of formalized, comprehensive, and exercised intrastate mutual-aid plans.

- **IAFC Fire Service Mutual-Aid System Task Force.** The task force is charged with developing a plan for an intrastate mutual aid system. Once completed, the system plans will support the Mutual-Aid System Task Force plan, creating a mutual-aid system that will cover the continental United States.

- **IAFC/IAFF National Fire Fighter Near-Miss Reporting System Task Force.** This program encourages firefighters to help improve safety practices and equipment by sharing near-miss experiences so that all firefighters and emergency responders can help prevent injuries and fatalities.

- **International Association of Chiefs of Police (IACP) Research Center.** The center identifies issues in law enforcement and conducts timely policy research, performs evaluations, and provides follow-up training and technical assistance for law enforcement leaders, the justice system, and the community. The center also hosts national summits on issues relevant to the law enforcement community.

- **IACP Center for Police Leadership.** This is a training and resource center for police departments around the world, providing fee-based, on-site training and technical assistance, and developing leadership publications that are academic but practical.

- **IACP DuPont KEVLAR Survivors' Club.** The club recognizes officers whose lives have been saved by wearing soft body armor. This encourages continual wearing of the armor by officers and provides local police departments with useful information and the opportunity to reinforce the importance of wearing soft body armor.

- **National Sheriffs' Association Weapons of Mass Destruction (WMD) Training.** The curriculum provides free WMD training for the Nation's sheriffs to strengthen their ability to effectively respond to WMD incidents. Courses include Community Awareness and Partnership Training (educating community groups to prepare for a WMD attack), Jail Evacuation and Implementation (preparing for facility evacuation in the event of a terrorist attack or all-hazards event), First-Responder Training (focusing on the actions required in the initial phase of a WMD response), and Managing the Incident Executive Level Training for Sheriffs.

- **International Association of Bomb Technicians and Investigators.** This is an independent, nonprofit, professional association formed to counter the criminal use of explosives. Objectives are attained through exchange of training, expertise, and information among personnel employed in the fields of law enforcement, fire and emergency services, military, forensic science, and other related fields.

- **National Bomb Squad Commanders Advisory Board.** The board serves as the leadership element of the U.S. Bomb Squad program, providing advice to Federal agencies that support bomb squads and acting as the final decision-making authority on guidelines and standards for the profession.

- **National Emergency Management Association (NEMA).** This consortium provides a forum for key national organizations to effectively communicate, collaborate, and coordinate in order to positively promote national policies, strategies, practices and guidelines to preserve public health, safety, and security.

- **System Assessment and Validation for Emergency Responders Program.** The program provides impartial, practitioner-relevant, and operationally oriented assessments and validations of emergency responder equipment; provides information that enables decision makers and responders to better select, procure, use, and maintain equipment; assesses and validates the performance of products within a system, as well as systems within systems; and provides information and feedback to the user community through a well-maintained, Web-based database.

Grant Programs

There are numerous Federal grant programs to assist the ESS in protecting CIKR, as well as enhancing the Nation's security in an all-hazards environment. The following are some of the Federal grant programs that enhance the CIKR protection efforts of the ESS:

- **State Homeland Security Grant Program.** This program provides funds to enhance State and local governments' capabilities to prevent, deter, respond to, and recover from incidents of terrorism involving CBRNE weapons and cyber attacks.

- **Urban Areas Security Initiative.** This initiative addresses the unique equipment, training, planning, and exercise needs of large, high-threat urban areas. Funding is provided for select urban areas and nonprofit organizations.

- **BZPP Grants.** BZPP provides funding to build security and risk management capabilities at the State and local levels to secure critical infrastructure including chemical facilities, nuclear and electric power plants, dams, stadiums, arenas, and other high-risk areas.

- **Competitive Training Grants Program.** This program provides funding for training initiatives to prepare the Nation in the event of a terrorist attack.

- **Interoperable Emergency Communications Grant Program (IECGP).** IECGP is being administered as a joint effort between DHS Office of Emergency Communications (OEC) and FEMA Grant Programs Directorate (GPD). IECGP helps State, local, tribal, and territorial governments to improve interoperable emergency communications, including communications in collective response to natural disasters, acts of terrorism, and other manmade disasters.

- **Metropolitan Medical Response System Program (MMRS).** The MMRS supports the integration of emergency management, health, and medical systems into a coordinated response to mass casualty incidents caused by any hazard. Successful MMRS grantees reduce the consequences of a mass casualty incident during the initial period of a response by having augmented existing local operational response systems before the incident occurs.

- **Emergency Management Performance Grants (EMPG).** The purpose of the Fiscal Year 2009 (FY 2009) EMPG was to assist State and local governments in enhancing and sustaining all-hazards emergency management capabilities.

- **Staffing for Adequate Fire and Emergency Response (SAFER) Grant.** The SAFER Grant was created to provide funding directly to fire departments and volunteer firefighter interest organizations in order to help them increase the number of trained, frontline firefighters available in their communities. The goal of SAFER is to enhance the local fire departments' abilities to comply with staffing, response, and operational standards established by the National Fire Protection Association (NFPA) and the Occupational Safety and Health Administration (OSHA).

- **Fire Prevention and Safety (FP&S) Grants.** FP&S grants support projects that enhance the safety of the public and firefighters from fire and related hazards. The primary goal is to target high-risk populations and firefighter safety, and mitigate high incidences of death and injury. In FY 2005, Congress reauthorized funding for FP&S and expanded the eligible uses of funds to include Firefighter Safety Research and Development.

- **CIKR Asset Protection Technical Assistance Program (CAPTAP).** CAPTAP is offered jointly by DHS IP and FEMA's National Preparedness Directorate (NPD) to assist State and local first responders, emergency managers, and homeland security officials understand the basic tenets of the NIPP, the value of a comprehensive State and local infrastructure protection program, and the steps required to develop and implement such a program.

- **Commercial Equipment Direct Assistance Program (CEDAP).** CEDAP complements FEMA NPD's other major grant programs to enhance regional response capabilities, mutual aid, and interoperable communications by providing technology and equipment, together with training and technical assistance required to operate that equipment, to public safety agencies in smaller jurisdictions and certain metropolitan areas.

- **Fire Management Assistance Grant Program.** This program provides assistance for the mitigation, management, and control of fires on publicly or privately owned forests or grasslands, which threaten such destruction as would constitute a major disaster.

- **State Fire Training System Grants.** State Fire Training System Grants provide financial assistance to State Fire Training Systems for the delivery of a variety of National Fire Academy courses and programs.

Appendix 4: Cyber Programs

In recognition of the potential adverse impact to the sector should its cyber assets and systems be targeted, the ESS participates in many programs designed to identify emergent threats, protect vital systems, and mitigate the impact of a cyber event. Examples of sector cyber programs follow:

- **Control Systems Security Program (CSSP).** The CSSP coordinates activities among Federal, State, local, and tribal governments, as well as control systems owners, operators, and vendors to reduce the likelihood of success and severity of impact of a cyber attack against CIKR control systems through risk mitigation activities;

- **Critical Infrastructure Protection: Cyber Security Program (CIP CS).** In partnership with public and private sectors, CIP CS helps improve the security of the IT Sector and cyberspace across U.S. CIKR sectors by facilitating risk reduction through infrastructure identification, vulnerability assessment, and protective measures initiatives;

- **Cross-Sector Cyber Security Working Group (CSCSWG).** The CSCSWG was established to improve cross-sector cybersecurity protection efforts across the Nation's CIKR sectors by identifying opportunities to improve sector coordination around cybersecurity issues and topics, highlighting cyber dependencies and interdependencies, and sharing government and private sector cybersecurity products and findings;

- **Cyber Exercise Program (CEP).** CEP improves the Nation's cybersecurity readiness, protection, and incident response capabilities by developing, designing, and conducting cyber exercises and workshops at the Federal, State, regional, and international level. CEP employs scenario-based exercises that focus on risks to the cyber and information technology infrastructure;

- **Software Assurance Program.** The Software Assurance Program seeks to reduce software vulnerabilities, minimize exploitation, and address ways to improve the routine development and deployment of trustworthy software products. These activities enable more secure and reliable software that supports the Nation's CIKR; and

- **U. S. Computer Emergency Readiness Team (US-CERT).** US-CERT is the U.S. Government's principal cyber watch and warning center. It is responsible for analyzing and reducing cyber threats and vulnerabilities; disseminating cyber threat warning information; and coordinating incident response activities. US-CERT interacts with Federal agencies, industry, the research community, State and local governments, and others to disseminate reasoned and actionable cybersecurity information.

Appendix 5: Capability Gaps

In 2009, the sector submitted technology requirements to the DHS Science and Technology Directorate (S&T) based on input from sector partners. From these technology requirements, the sector identified seven capability gaps, of which two were approved, four require further review by the Research & Development Working Group (RDWG), and one was transferred to the National Institute for Hometown Security.

Table A5-1: Progress on 2008 Capability Gap/Mission Need Statements

Statement Tracking Number	2008-001-Emergency Services
Requirement Title	Occupational Safety and Health Research
Action	Requires nonmaterial solution that cannot be achieved through research and development (R&D).
Status	This capability gap will be reassessed as a possible mission need by the RDWG. If a specific operational requirement can be created out of this assessment, it will be forwarded to S&T. This capability gap is also being pursued by the Institute of Medicine.

Statement Tracking Number	2008-002-Emergency Services
Requirement Title	Simulating Emergency Services Response and Recovery for Pandemic Influenza
Action	Submitted to National Institute for Hometown Security.
Status	Gap was combined with 2008-001-Health (Informatics: Secure Information Exchange for Medical Surge Capacity), 2008-002-Health (Crisis Standards of Care), 2008-004-Health (Health Systems Capacity Management), 2008-005-Health (Healthcare and Public Health Workforce Protection: Ensuring Mental Health Before, During, and After a Crisis) into one project, the title of which is still to be determined. Request for Proposals deadline was January 30, 2009.

Statement Tracking Number	2008-003-Emergency Services
Requirement Title	First Responder Chemical, Biological, Radiological, Nuclear, and High-Yield Explosives (CBRNE) Equipment Standards
Action	Requires nonmaterial solution that cannot be achieved through R&D.
Status	This capability gap will be reassessed as a possible mission need by the Research & Development Working Group (RDWG). If a specific operational requirement can be created out of this assessment, it will be forwarded to S&T. This capability gap is also being pursued by the InterAgency Board.

Statement Tracking Number	2008-004-Emergency Services
Requirement Title	Equipment Positioning Modeling
Action	Submitted to Incident Management Preparation and Response Capstone Integrated Product Team (IM IPT).
Status	This capability gap will be reassessed by the Incident Management Preparation and Response Capstone Integrated Product Team (IM IPT).

Statement Tracking Number	2008-005-Emergency Services
Requirement Title	Enhanced Training Modules
Action	Requires nonmaterial solution that cannot be achieved through R&D.
Status	This capability gap will be reassessed by the Research and Development Working Group. If a specific operational requirement can be created out of this assessment, it will be forwarded to S&T.

Statement Tracking Number	2008-008-Chemical
Requirement Title	Emergency Services and Private Vehicle Operation within a Large, Life-Threatening Toxic Vapor Cloud of Chlorine
Action	Submitted to S&T ChemBio Division.
Status	A system study will be conducted for this capability gap in Fiscal Year 2010.

Appendix 6: Summary of Relevant Authorities, Statutes, Strategies, and Directives

This appendix provides information on the governing authorities most relevant to protecting ESS assets, systems, networks, and functions.

Many of the definitions in this glossary are derived from language used in Federal laws or included in national plans. Sources include the Homeland Security Act of 2002, the Uniting and Strengthening America by Providing Appropriate Tools Required to Intercept and Obstruct Terrorism Act (USA PATRIOT Act) of 2001, the NIPP, NIMS, and the NRF.

This summary provides additional information on a variety of statutes, strategies, and directives referenced in chapters 2 and 5, as applicable to CIKR protection. This list is not inclusive of all authorities related to CIKR protection; rather, it includes the authorities most relevant to national-level, cross-sector CIKR protection. Please note that there are many other authorities that are related to specific sectors that are not discussed in this appendix. These are left for further elaboration in the SSPs.

Statutes

Homeland Security Act of 2002. This act establishes a Cabinet-level department headed by a Secretary of Homeland Security with the mandate and legal authority to protect the American people from the continuing threat of terrorism. In the act, Congress assigns DHS the primary missions to:

- Prevent terrorist attacks within the United States;

- Reduce the vulnerability of the United States to terrorism at home;

- Minimize the damage and assist in the recovery from terrorist attacks that occur; and

- Ensure that the overall economic security of the United States is not diminished by efforts, activities, and programs aimed at securing the homeland.

This statutory authority defines the protection of CIKR as one of the primary missions of the Department. Among other actions, the act specifically requires DHS to:

- Carry out comprehensive assessments of the vulnerabilities of the CIKR of the United States, including the performance of risk assessments to determine the risks posed by particular types of terrorist attacks;

- Develop a comprehensive national plan for securing the key resources and critical infrastructure of the United States, including power production, generation, and distribution systems; information technology and telecommunications systems (including satellites); electronic financial and property record storage and transmission systems; emergency preparedness communications systems; and the physical and technological assets that support such systems; and

- Recommend measures necessary to protect the CIKR of the United States in coordination with other agencies of the Federal Government and in cooperation with State and local government agencies and authorities, the private sector, and other entities.

These requirements, combined with the President's direction in HSPD-7, mandate the unified approach to CIKR protection taken in the NIPP.

Critical Infrastructure Information Act of 2002. Enacted as part of the Homeland Security Act, this act creates a framework that enables members of the private sector and others to voluntarily submit sensitive information regarding the Nation's CIKR to DHS with the assurance that the information, if it satisfies certain requirements, will be protected from public disclosure.

The PCII Program, created under the authority of the act, is central to the information-sharing and protection strategy of the NIPP. By protecting sensitive information submitted through the program, the private sector is assured that the information will remain secure and be used only to further CIKR protection efforts.

Implementing Recommendations of the 9/11 Commission Act of 2007. This act requires the implementation of some of the recommendations made by the 9/11 Commission to include requirements for the Secretary of Homeland Security to: (1) establish Department-wide procedures to receive and analyze intelligence from State, local, and tribal governments and the private sector; and (2) establish a system that screens 100 percent of maritime and passenger cargo.

This act establishes the International Border Community Interoperable Communications Demonstration Project to help identify and implement solutions to cross-border communications and cooperation, and the Interagency Threat Assessment and Coordination Group (ITACG), to improve inter-agency communications. The establishment of ITACG Advisory Councils allows Federal agencies to set policies to improve communication within the information-sharing environment and supports establishment of an ITACG Detail that gives State, local, and tribal homeland security officials, law enforcement officers, and intelligence analysts the opportunity to work in the National Counterterrorism Center.

The Act also established grants to support high-risk urban areas and State, local, and tribal governments in preventing, preparing for, protecting against, and responding to acts of terrorism, and to assist States in carrying out initiatives to improve international emergency communications.

Robert T. Stafford Disaster Relief and Emergency Assistance Act (Stafford Act). The Stafford Act provides comprehensive authority for response to emergencies and major disasters—natural disasters, accidents, and intentionally perpetrated events. It provides specific authority for the Federal Government to provide assistance to State and local entities for disaster preparedness and mitigation, and major disaster and emergency assistance. Major disaster and emergency assistance includes such resources and services as:

- Provision of Federal resources, in general
- Medicine, food, and other consumables
- Work and services to save lives and restore property, including:
  - Debris removal
  - Search and rescue; emergency medical care; emergency mass care; emergency shelter; and provision of food, water, medicine, and other essential needs, including movement of supplies or persons
  - Clearance of roads and construction of temporary bridges
  - Provision of temporary facilities for schools and other essential community services
  - Demolition of unsafe structures that endanger the public
  - Warning of further risks and hazards

- Dissemination of public information and assistance regarding health and safety measures

- Provision of technical advice to State and local governments on disaster management and control

- Reduction of immediate threats to life, property, and public health and safety

• Hazard mitigation

• Repair, replacement, and restoration of certain damaged facilities

• Emergency communications, emergency transportation, and fire management assistance

Disaster Mitigation Act of 2000. This act amends the Stafford Act by repealing the previous mitigation planning provisions (section 409) and replacing them with a new set of requirements (section 322). This new section emphasizes the need for State, local, and tribal entities to closely coordinate mitigation planning and implementation efforts.

Section 322 continues the requirement for a State mitigation plan as a condition of disaster assistance, adding incentives for increased coordination and integration of mitigation activities at the State level through the establishment of requirements for two different levels of State plans—standard and enhanced. States that demonstrate an increased commitment to comprehensive mitigation planning and implementation through the development of an approved Enhanced State Plan can increase the amount of funding available through the Hazard Mitigation Grant Program (HMGP). Section 322 also established a new requirement for local mitigation plans and authorized up to 7 percent of HMGP funds available to a State to be used for development of State, local, and tribal mitigation plans.

Corporate and Criminal Fraud Accountability Act of 2002 (also known as the Sarbanes-Oxley Act). The act applies to entities required to file periodic reports with the Securities and Exchange Commission under the provisions of the Securities and Exchange Act of 1934, as amended. It contains significant changes to the responsibilities of directors and officers, as well as the reporting and corporate governance obligations of affected companies. Among other things, the act requires certification by the company's chief executive officer and chief financial officer that accompanies each periodic report filed that the report fully complies with the requirements of the securities laws and that the information in the report fairly presents, in all material respects, the financial condition and results of the operations of the company. It also requires certifications regarding internal controls and material misstatements or omissions, and the disclosure on a "rapid and current basis" of information regarding material changes in the financial condition or operations of a public company. The act contains a number of additional provisions dealing with insider accountability and disclosure obligations, and auditor independence. It also provides severe criminal and civil penalties for violations of the act's provisions.

The Defense Production Act of 1950 and the Defense Production Reauthorization Act of 2009. This act provides the primary authority to ensure the timely availability of resources for national defense and civil emergency preparedness and response. Among other powers, this act authorizes the President to demand that companies accept and give priority to government contracts that the President "deems necessary or appropriate to promote the national defense," and allocate materials, services, and facilities, as necessary, to promote the national defense in a major national emergency. This act also authorizes loan guarantees, direct loans, direct purchases, and purchase guarantees for those goods necessary for national defense. It also allows the President to void international mergers that would adversely affect national security. This act defines "national defense" to include critical infrastructure protection and restoration, as well as activities authorized by the emergency preparedness sections of the Stafford Act. Consequently, the authorities stemming from the Defense Production Act are available for activities and measures undertaken in preparation for, during, or following a natural disaster or accidental or malicious event. Under the act and related Presidential orders, the Secretary of Homeland Security has the authority to place and, upon application, authorize State and local governments to place priority-rated contracts in support of Federal, State, and local emergency preparedness activities. The Defense Production Act has a national security nexus with the NIPP. National emergencies related to CIKR may arise that require the President to use his authority under the Defense Production Act.

The Posse Comitatus Act. This Act, 18 U.S.C. 1385, prohibits use of the Army or Air Force for law enforcement purposes, except as otherwise authorized by the Constitution or statute. This prohibition applies to Navy and Marine Corps personnel as a matter of DoD policy. The primary prohibition of the Posse Comitatus Act is against direct involvement by active duty military personnel (to include reservists on active duty and National Guard personnel in Federal service) in traditional law enforcement activities (to include interdiction of vehicle, vessel, aircraft, or other similar activity; directing traffic; search or seizure; an arrest, apprehension, stop and frisk, or similar activity).

The Freedom of Information Act (FOIA). This act generally provides that any person has a right, enforceable in court, to obtain access to Federal agency records, except to the extent that such records are protected from public disclosure by nine listed exemptions or under three law enforcement exclusions.

Persons who make requests are not required to identify themselves or explain the purpose of the request. The underlying principle of FOIA is that the workings of government are for and by the people and that the benefits of government information should be made broadly available. All Federal Government agencies must adhere to the provisions of FOIA with certain exceptions for work in progress, enforcement confidential information, classified documents, and national security information. FOIA was amended by the Electronic Freedom of Information Act Amendment of 1996.

Information Technology Management Reform Act of 1996. Under section 5131 of the Information Technology Management Reform Act of 1996, the National Institute of Standards and Technology (NIST) develops standards, guidelines, and associated methods and techniques for Federal computer systems. Federal Information Processing Standards are developed by NIST only when there are no existing voluntary standards to address the Federal requirements for the interoperability of different systems, the portability of data and software, and computer security.

Gramm-Leach-Bliley Act of 1999. Among other things, this act (Title V) provides limited privacy protections on the disclosure by a financial institution of nonpublic personal information. The act also codifies protections against the practice of obtaining personal information through false pretenses.

Public Health Security and Bioterrorism Preparedness and Response Act of 2002. This act improves the ability of the United States to prevent, prepare for, and respond to bioterrorism and other public health emergencies. Key provisions of the act, 42 U.S.C. 247d and 300hh among others, address: (1) development of a national preparedness plan by HHS that is designed to provide effective assistance to State and local governments in the event of bioterrorism or other public health emergencies; (2) operation of the National Disaster Medical System to mobilize and address public health emergencies; (3) grant programs for the education and training of public health professionals and the improvement of State, local, and hospital preparedness for and response to bioterrorism and other public health emergencies; (4) streamlining and clarification of communicable disease quarantine provisions; (5) enhancement of controls on dangerous biological agents and toxins; and (6) protection of the safety and security of food and drug supplies.

Uniting and Strengthening America by Providing Appropriate Tools Required to Intercept and Obstruct Terrorism (USA PATRIOT Act) of 2001. This act outlines the domestic policy related to deterring and punishing terrorists, and the U.S. policy for CIKR protection. It also provides for the establishment of a national competence for CIKR protection. The act establishes the National Infrastructure Simulation and Analysis Center and outlines the Federal Government's commitment to understanding and protecting the interdependencies among critical infrastructure.

The Privacy Act of 1974. This act provides strict limits on the maintenance and disclosure by any Federal agency of information on individuals that is maintained, including "education, financial transactions, medical history, and criminal or employment history and that contains [the] name, or the identifying number, symbol, or other identifying particular assigned to the individual, such as a finger or voice print or a photograph." Although there are specific categories for permissible maintenance of records and limited exceptions to the prohibition on disclosure for legitimate law enforcement and other specified purposes, the act requires strict recordkeeping on any disclosure. The act also specifically provides for access by individuals to their own records and for requesting corrections thereto.

Federal Information Security Management Act of 2002. This act requires that Federal agencies develop a comprehensive information technology security program to ensure the effectiveness of information security controls over information resources that support Federal operations and assets. This legislation is relevant to the part of the NIPP that governs the protection of Federal assets and the implementation of cyber-protective measures under the Government Facilities SSP.

Cyber Security Research and Development Act of 2002. This act allocates funding to NIST and the National Science Foundation for the purpose of facilitating increased R&D for computer network security and supporting research fellowships and training. The act establishes a means of enhancing basic R&D related to improving the cybersecurity of CIKR.

Maritime Transportation Security Act of 2002. This act directs initial and continuing assessments of maritime facilities and vessels that may be involved in a transportation security incident. It requires DHS to prepare a National Maritime Transportation Security Plan for deterring and responding to a transportation security incident and to prepare incident response plans for facilities and vessels that will ensure effective coordination with Federal, State, and local authorities. It also requires, among other actions, the establishment of transportation security and crewmember identification cards and processes; maritime safety and security teams; port security grants; and enhancements to maritime intelligence and matters dealing with foreign ports and international cooperation.

Intelligence Reform and Terrorism Prevention Act of 2004. This act provides sweeping changes to the U.S. Intelligence Community structure and processes, and creates new systems specially designed to combat terrorism. Among other actions, the act:

- Establishes a Director of National Intelligence with specific budget, oversight, and programmatic authority over the Intelligence Community;

- Establishes the National Intelligence Council and redefines "national intelligence";

- Requires the establishment of a secure ISE and an information-sharing council;

- Establishes a National Counterterrorism Center, a National Counterproliferation Center, National Intelligence Centers, and a Joint Intelligence Community Council;

- Establishes, within the Executive Office of the President, a Privacy and Civil Liberties Oversight Board;

- Requires the Director of the FBI to continue efforts to improve the intelligence capabilities of the FBI and to develop and maintain, within the FBI, a national intelligence workforce;

- Directs improvements in security clearances and clearance processes;

- Requires DHS to develop and implement a National Strategy for Transportation Security and transportation modal security plans; enhance identification and credentialing of transportation workers and law enforcement officers; conduct R&D into mass identification technology, including biometrics; enhance passenger screening and terrorist watch lists; improve measures for detecting weapons and explosives; improve security related to the air transportation of cargo; and implement other aviation security measures;

- Directs enhancements to maritime security;

- Directs enhancements in border security and immigration matters;

- Enhances law enforcement authority and capabilities, and expands certain diplomatic, foreign aid, and military authorities and capabilities for combating terrorism;

- Requires expanded machine-readable visas with biometric data; implementation of a biometric entry and exit system, and a registered traveler program; and implementation of biometric or other secure passports;

- Requires standards for birth certificates and driver's licenses or personal identification cards issued by States for use by Federal agencies for identification purposes, and enhanced regulations for social security cards;

- Requires DHS to improve preparedness nationally, especially measures to enhance interoperable communications, and to report on vulnerability and risk assessments of the Nation's CIKR; and

- Directs measures to improve assistance to and coordination with State, local, and private sector entities.

National Strategies

National Strategy for Homeland Security (October 2007). The updated strategy serves to guide, organize, and unify our Nation's homeland security efforts. It is a national strategy, not a Federal strategy that articulates the approach to secure the homeland over the next several years. It builds on the first National Strategy for Homeland Security, issued in July 2002, and complements both the National Security Strategy, issued in March 2006, and the National Strategy for Combating Terrorism, issued in September 2006. It reflects the increased understanding of threats confronting the United States, incorporates lessons learned from exercises and real-world catastrophes, and addresses ways to ensure long-term success by strengthening the homeland security foundation that has been built.

The National Strategy for Homeland Security (July 2002). This strategy establishes the Nation's strategic homeland security objectives and outlines the six critical mission areas necessary to achieve those objectives. The strategy also provides a framework to align the resources of the Federal budget directly to the task of securing the homeland. The strategy specifies eight major initiatives to protect the Nation's CIKR, one of which specifically calls for the development of the NIPP.

National Strategy for the Physical Protection of Critical Infrastructures and Key Assets (February 2003). This strategy identifies the policy, goals, objectives, and principles for actions needed to "secure the infrastructures and assets vital to national security, governance, public health and safety, economy, and public confidence." The strategy provides a unifying organizational structure for CIKR protection and identifies specific initiatives related to the NIPP to drive near-term national protection priorities and inform the resource allocation process.

National Strategy to Secure Cyberspace (February 2003). This strategy sets forth objectives and specific actions to prevent cyber attacks against America's CIKR, reduce nationally identified vulnerabilities to cyber attacks, and minimize damage and recovery time from cyber attacks. The strategy provides the vision for cybersecurity and serves as the foundation for the cybersecurity component of CIKR.

The National Strategy for Maritime Security (September 2005). This strategy provides the framework to integrate and synchronize the existing Department-level strategies and ensure their effective and efficient implementation, and aligns all Federal Government maritime security programs and initiatives into a comprehensive and cohesive national effort involving appropriate Federal, State, local, and private sector entities.

The National Strategy to Combat Weapons of Mass Destruction (December 2002). This strategy provides policy guidance on combating WMD through three pillars:

- Counter proliferation to combat WMD use;

- Strengthened nonproliferation to combat WMD proliferation; and

- Consequence management to respond to WMD use.

The National Strategy for Combating Terrorism (February 2003). This strategy provides a comprehensive overview of the terrorist threat and sets specific goals and objectives to combat this threat, including measures to:

- Defeat terrorists and their organizations;

- Deny sponsorship, support, and sanctuary to terrorists;

- Diminish the underlying conditions that terrorists seek to exploit; and

- Defend U.S. citizens and interests at home and abroad.

The National Intelligence Strategy of the United States of America. The National Intelligence Strategy of the United States of America outlines the fundamental values, priorities, and orientation of the Intelligence Community. As directed by the Director of National Intelligence, the strategy outlines the specific mission objectives that relate to efforts to predict, penetrate, and preempt threats to national security. To accomplish this, the efforts of the different enterprises of the Intelligence Community are integrated through policy, doctrine, and technology, and by ensuring that intelligence efforts are appropriately coordinated with the Nation's homeland security mission.

Homeland Security Presidential Directives

HSPD-1: Organization and Operation of the Homeland Security Council (October 2001). HSPD-1 establishes the Homeland Security Council and a committee structure for developing, coordinating, and vetting homeland security policy among executive departments and agencies. The directive provides a mandate for the Homeland Security Council to ensure the coordination of all homeland security-related activities among executive departments and agencies, and promotes the effective development and implementation of all homeland security policies. The Homeland Security Council is responsible for arbitrating and coordinating any policy issues that may arise among the different departments and agencies under the NIPP.

HSPD-2: Combating Terrorism Through Immigration Policies (October 2001). HSPD-2 establishes policies and programs to enhance the Federal Government's capabilities for preventing aliens who engage in or support terrorist activities from entering the country, and for detaining, prosecuting, or deporting any such aliens who are in the United States.

HSPD-2 also directs the Attorney General to create the Foreign Terrorist Tracking Task Force to ensure that, to the maximum extent permitted by law, Federal agencies coordinate programs to accomplish the following: (1) deny entry into the United States of aliens associated with, suspected of being engaged in, or supporting terrorist activity; and (2) locate, detain, prosecute, or deport any such aliens already present in the United States.

HSPD-3: Homeland Security Advisory System (March 2002). HSPD-3 mandates the creation of an alert system for disseminating information regarding the risk of terrorist acts to Federal, State, and local authorities, and the public. It also includes the requirement for a corresponding set of protective measures for Federal, State, and local governments to be implemented, depending on the threat condition. Such a system provides warnings in the form of a set of graduated threat conditions that are elevated as the risk of the threat increases. For each threat condition, Federal departments and agencies are required to implement a corresponding set of protective measures.

HSPD-4: National Strategy to Combat Weapons of Mass Destruction (December 2002). This directive outlines a strategy that includes three principal pillars: (1) Counter-Proliferation to Combat WMD Use, (2) Strengthened Nonproliferation to Combat WMD Proliferation, and (3) Consequence Management to Respond to WMD Use. It also outlines four cross-cutting functions to be pursued on a priority basis: (1) intelligence collection and analysis on WMD, delivery systems, and related technologies; (2) R&D to improve our ability to address evolving threats; (3) bilateral and multilateral cooperation; and (4) targeted strategies against hostile nations and terrorists.

HSPD-5: Management of Domestic Incidents (February 2003). HSPD-5 establishes a national approach to domestic incident management that ensures effective coordination among all levels of government, and between the government and the private sector. Central to this approach is NIMS, an organizational framework for all levels of government, and NRF, an operational framework for national incident response. In this directive, the President designates the Secretary of Homeland Security as the principal Federal official for domestic incident management and empowers the Secretary to coordinate Federal resources used for prevention, preparedness, response, and recovery related to terrorist attacks, major disasters, or other emergencies. The directive assigns specific responsibilities to the Attorney General, Secretary of Defense, Secretary of State, and the Assistants to the President for Homeland Security and National Security Affairs, and directs the heads of all Federal departments and agencies to provide their "full and prompt cooperation, resources, and support," as appropriate and consistent with their own responsibilities for protecting national security, to the Secretary of Homeland Security, Attorney General, Secretary of Defense, and Secretary of State in the exercise of leadership responsibilities and missions assigned in HSPD-5.

HSPD-6: Integration and Use of Screening Information (September 2003). HSPD-6 consolidates the Federal Government's approach to terrorist screening by establishing a Terrorist Screening Center. Federal departments and agencies are directed to provide terrorist information to the Terrorist Threat Integration Center, which is then required to provide all relevant information and intelligence to the Terrorist Screening Center. In order to protect against terrorism, this directive established the national policy to: (1) develop, integrate, and maintain thorough, accurate, and current information about individuals known or appropriately suspected to be or have been engaged in conduct constituting, in preparation for, in aid of, or related to terrorism (Terrorist Information); and (2) use that information, as appropriate and to the full extent permitted by law, to support (a) Federal, State, local, territorial, tribal, foreign government, and private sector screening processes; and (b) diplomatic, military, intelligence, law enforcement, immigration, visa, and protective processes.

HSPD-7: Critical Infrastructure Identification, Prioritization, and Protection (December 2003). HSPD-7 establishes a framework for Federal departments and agencies to identify, prioritize, and protect CIKR from terrorist attacks, with an emphasis on protecting against catastrophic health effects and mass casualties. HSPD-7 mandates the creation and implementation of the NIPP and sets forth roles and responsibilities for DHS; Sector-Specific Agencies; other Federal departments and agencies; and State, local, tribal, territorial, private sector, and other CIKR partners.

HSPD-8: National Preparedness (December 2003). HSPD-8 establishes policies to strengthen the preparedness of the United States to prevent, protect, respond to, and recover from threatened or actual domestic terrorist attacks, major disasters, and other emergencies by requiring a national domestic all-hazards preparedness goal; establishing mechanisms for improved delivery of Federal preparedness assistance to State and local governments; and outlining actions to strengthen the preparedness capabilities of Federal, State, and local entities. This directive mandates the development of the goal to guide emergency preparedness training, planning, equipment, and exercises, and to ensure that all entities involved adhere to the same standards. The directive calls for an inventory of Federal response capabilities and refines the process by which preparedness grants are administered, disbursed, and utilized at the State and local levels.

HSPD-9: Defense of United States Agriculture and Food (January 2004). HSPD-9 establishes an integrated national policy for improving intelligence operations, emergency response capabilities, information-sharing mechanisms, mitigation strategies, and sector vulnerability assessments to defend the agriculture and food system against terrorist attacks, major disasters, and other emergencies.

HSPD-10: Biodefense for the 21st Century (April 2004). HSPD-10 outlines the essential pillars of our national biodefense program as threat awareness, prevention and protection, surveillance and detection, and response and recovery. This directive describes these various disciplines in detail and sets forth objectives for further progress under the national biodefense program, highlighting key roles for Federal departments and agencies. The Secretary of Homeland Security is responsible for coordinating domestic Federal operations to prepare for, respond to, and recover from biological weapons attacks.

HSPD-11: Comprehensive Terrorist-Related Screening Procedures (August 2004). HSPD-11 requires the creation of a strategy and implementation plan for a coordinated and comprehensive approach to terrorist screening to improve and expand procedures to screen people, cargo, conveyances, and other entities and objects that pose a threat.

HSPD-12: Policy for a Common Identification for Federal Employees and Contractors (August 2004). HSPD-12 establishes a mandatory, government-wide standard for secure and reliable forms of identification issued by the Federal Government to its employees and contractors to enhance security, increase government efficiency, reduce identity fraud, and protect personal privacy. The resulting mandatory standard was issued by NIST as the Federal Information Processing Standard Publication.

HSPD-13: Maritime Security Policy (December 2004). HSPD-13 directs the coordination of U.S. Government maritime security programs and initiatives to achieve a comprehensive and cohesive national effort involving the appropriate Federal, State, local, and private sector entities. The directive also establishes a Maritime Security Policy Coordinating Committee to coordinate inter-agency maritime security policy efforts.

HSPD-14: Domestic Nuclear Detection (April 2005). HSPD-14 establishes the effective integration of nuclear and radiological detection capabilities across Federal, State, local, and tribal governments and the private sector for a managed, coordinated response. This directive supports and enhances the effective sharing and use of appropriate information generated by the intelligence community, law enforcement agencies, counterterrorism community, other government agencies, and foreign governments, as well as providing appropriate information to these entities.

HSPD-15: War on Terror (March 2006). HSPD-15 is classified but the objective of the directive is to improve government coordination in the global war on terror.

HSPD-16: Aviation Security Policy (June 2006). HSPD-16 details a strategic vision for aviation security while recognizing ongoing efforts, and directs the production of a National Strategy for Aviation Security and supporting plans. The supporting plans address the following areas: aviation transportation system security; aviation operational threat response; aviation transportation system recovery; air domain surveillance and intelligence integration; domestic outreach; and international outreach. The strategy sets forth U.S. Government agency roles and responsibilities, establishes planning and operations coordination requirements, and builds on current strategies, tools, and resources.

HSPD-17: Nuclear Materials Information Program (August 2006). The contents of HSPD-17 are classified. The directive addresses an inter-agency effort managed by the U.S. Department of Energy to consolidate information from all sources pertaining to worldwide nuclear materials holdings and their security status into an integrated and continuously updated information management system.

HSPD-18: Medical Countermeasures against Weapons of Mass Destruction (January 2007). HSPD-18 builds on the vision and objectives articulated in the National Strategy to Combat Weapons of Mass Destruction and Biodefense for the 21st Century to ensure that the Nation's medical countermeasure research, development, and acquisition efforts target threats for catastrophic impact on public health; yield a rapidly deployable and flexible capability to address existing and evolving threats; are part of an integrated WMD consequence management approach; and include the development of effective, feasible, and pragmatic concepts of operation for responding to and recovering from an attack. The directive designates the Secretary of Homeland Security to develop a strategic, integrated, all-CBRN risk assessment that integrates the findings of the intelligence and law enforcement communities with input from the scientific, medical, and public health communities.

HSPD-19: Combating Terrorist Use of Explosives in the United States (February 2007). HSPD-19 establishes a national policy, and calls for the development of a national strategy and implementation plan, on the prevention and detection of, protection against, and response to terrorist use of explosives in the United States. This directive mandates that the Secretary of Homeland Security coordinate with other Federal agencies to maintain secure information-sharing systems available to law enforcement agencies and other first responders, to include best practices to enhance preparedness across the government. The Secretary of Homeland Security is also responsible, in coordination with other Federal agencies, for Federal Government research, development, testing, and evaluation activities related to explosives attacks and the development of explosive render-safe tools and technologies.

HSPD-20: National Continuity Policy (May 2007). HSPD-20 establishes a comprehensive national policy on the continuity of Federal Government structures and operations and designates a single National Continuity Coordinator responsible for leading the development and implementation of Federal continuity policies. This policy establishes "National Essential Functions;" prescribes continuity requirements for all executive departments and agencies; and provides guidance for State, local, tribal, and territorial governments, and private sector organizations. This directive aims to ensure a comprehensive and integrated national continuity program that will enhance the credibility of our national security posture and enable a more rapid and effective response to and recovery from a national emergency.

HSPD-21: Public Health and Medical Preparedness (October 2007). HSPD-21 establishes a National Strategy for Public Health and Medical Preparedness. The Strategy draws key principles from the National Strategy for Homeland Security (October 2007), the National Strategy to Combat Weapons of Mass Destruction (December 2002), and Biodefense for the 21st Century (April 2004) that can be generally applied to public health and medical preparedness. Implementation of this strategy will transform our national approach to protecting the health of the American people against all disasters.

HSPD-23: Cyber Security and Monitoring (January 2008). The contents of HSPD-23 are classified. The directive establishes a task force, headed by the Office of the Director of National Intelligence, to identify the sources of cyber attacks against government computer systems.

HSPD-24: Biometrics for Identification and Screening to Enhance National Security (June 2008). HSPD-24 establishes a framework to ensure that Federal executive departments and agencies use mutually compatible methods and procedures in the collection, storage, use, analysis, and sharing of biometric and associated biographic and contextual information of individuals in a lawful and appropriate manner, while respecting their information privacy and other legal rights under U.S. law.

Other Authorities

Executive Order 13231, Critical Infrastructure Protection in the Information Age (October 2001) (amended by Executive Order 13286, February 28, 2003). This Executive Order provides specific policy direction to ensure protection of information systems for critical infrastructure, including emergency preparedness communications, and the physical assets that support such systems. It recognizes the important role that networked information systems (critical information infrastructure) play in supporting all aspects of our civil society and economy and the increasing degree to which other critical infrastructure sectors have become dependent on such systems. It formally establishes as U.S. policy the need to protect against disruption of the operation of these systems and to ensure that any disruptions that do occur are infrequent, of minimal duration, manageable, and cause the least damage possible. The Executive Order specifically calls for the implementation of the policy to include "a voluntary public-private partnership, involving corporate and nongovernmental organizations." The Executive Order also reaffirms existing authorities and responsibilities assigned to various executive branch agencies and inter-agency committees to ensure the security and integrity of Federal information systems generally and of national security information systems in particular.

National Infrastructure Advisory Council (NIAC). In addition to the foregoing, Executive Order 13231 (as amended by Executive Order 13286 of February 28, 2003, and Executive Order 13385 of September 29, 2005) also established the NIAC as the President's principal advisory panel on critical infrastructure protection issues spanning all sectors. The NIAC is composed of not more than 30 members, appointed by the President, who are selected from the private sector, academia, and State and local government, and represent senior executive leadership expertise from the critical infrastructure and key resource areas as delineated in HSPD-7.

The NIAC provides the President, through the Secretary of Homeland Security, with advice on the security of critical infrastructure, both physical and cyber, that support important sectors of the economy. It also has the authority to provide advice directly to the heads of other departments that have shared responsibility for critical infrastructure protection, including HHS, DOT, and DOE. The NIAC is charged to improve the cooperation and partnership between the public and private sectors in securing critical infrastructure and advises on policies and strategies that range from risk assessment and management, to information sharing, to protective strategies and clarification on roles and responsibilities between public and private sectors.

Executive Order 12382, President's National Security Telecommunications Advisory Committee (NSTAC), amended by Executive Order 13286, February 28, 2003. This Executive Order creates the NSTAC, which provides to the President, through the Secretary of Homeland Security, information and advice from the perspective of the telecommunications industry with respect to the implementation of the National Security Telecommunications Policy.

Executive Order 12472, Assignment of National Security and Emergency Preparedness Telecommunications Functions (amended by Executive Order 13286, February 28, 2003). Executive Order 12472 assigns NS/EP telecommunications functions, including wartime and non-wartime emergency functions, to the National Security Council, OSTP, Homeland Security Council, OMB, and other Federal agencies. The Executive Order seeks to ensure that the Federal Government has telecommunications services that will function under all conditions, including emergency situations. This Executive Order establishes the NCS with the mission to assist the President, the National Security Council, the Homeland Security Council, the Director of OSTP, and the Director of OMB in: (1) the exercise of telecommunications functions and responsibilities set forth in the Executive Order; and (2) the coordination of planning for and provision of NS/EP communications for the Federal Government under all circumstances, including crisis or emergency, attack, recovery, and reconstitution.

The Insurrection Statutes, 10 U.S.C. 331-334. Recognizing that the primary responsibility for protecting life and property and maintaining law and order in the civilian community is vested in State and local governments, the Insurrection Statutes authorize the President to direct the Armed Forces to enforce the law to suppress insurrections and domestic violence. Military forces may be used to restore order, prevent looting, and engage in other law enforcement activities. Given this specific statutory authority, the Posse Comitatus Act does not apply to such civil disturbance missions.

The Defense Against Weapons of Mass Destruction Act, 50 U.S.C. 2301. This Act is intended to enhance the capability of the Federal Government to prevent and respond to terrorist incidents involving WMD. Congress has directed DoD to provide enhanced support to improve the capabilities of State and local emergency response agencies to prevent and respond to WMD incidents at both the national and local levels. Support is to include domestic terrorism rapid response teams, training in emergency response to real or threatened use of WMD, and a program of testing and improving civil agencies' responses to biological and chemical emergencies.

Emergencies Involving Chemical or Biological Weapons, 10 U.S.C. 382. In response to an emergency involving biological or chemical WMD that is beyond the capabilities of civilian authorities to handle, the Attorney General may directly request DoD assistance. Assistance that may be provided includes monitoring, containing, disabling, and disposing of the weapon. Direct law enforcement assistance, such as conducting an arrest, searching or seizing evidence of criminal violations, or direct participation in collection of intelligence for law enforcement purposes, is not authorized unless it is necessary for immediate protection of human life, civilian law enforcement officials are not capable of taking the action, and the action is otherwise authorized.

Emergencies Involving Nuclear Materials, 18 U.S.C. 831(e). The Attorney General may request assistance from the Secretary of Defense under chapter 18 of title 10 in the enforcement of this section and the Secretary of Defense may provide such assistance in accordance with chapter 18 of title 10, except that the Secretary of Defense may provide such assistance through any U.S. Department of Defense personnel. This includes law enforcement assistance, including the authority to arrest and conduct searches, notwithstanding prohibitions of the Posse Comitatus Act, when both the Attorney General and Secretary of Defense agree that an "emergency situation" exists and the Secretary of Defense determines that the requested assistance will not impede military readiness. An emergency situation involving nuclear material is defined as a circumstance that poses a serious threat to the United States in which: (1) enforcement of the law would be seriously impaired if the assistance were not provided, and (2) civilian law enforcement personnel are not capable of enforcing the law. In addition, the statute authorizes

DoD personnel to engage in "such other activity as is incident to the enforcement of this section or to the protection of persons or property from conduct that violates this section."

Volunteer Services (includes statutory exceptions to the general statutory prohibition against accepting voluntary services under 31 U.S.C. 1342). Such services may be accepted in "emergencies involving the safety of human life or the protection of property." In addition, provisions of the Stafford Act, 42 U.S.C. 5152(a), 5170a (2), authorize the President to use the personnel of private disaster relief organizations and to coordinate their activities. Under the Congressional Charter of 1905 (36 U.S.C. 300101-300111 (codified 1998)), the American Red Cross and its chapters are a single national corporation organized to help fulfill U.S. treaty obligations under the Geneva Conventions. The charter mandates that the American Red Cross maintain a system of domestic and international disaster relief, and entrusts the organization to serve as a medium of communication between members of the military and their families. Consistent with the charter, the President of the United States appoints the chairman of the Board of Governors of the American Red Cross, as well as seven members of the Board, all of whom must be Federal Government officials. Congressional committees oversee the domestic and international activities of the American Red Cross. The U.S. Supreme Court has confirmed the legal status of the American Red Cross as a unique Federal instrumentality. The American Red Cross is recognized as a qualified tax-exempt 501(c)(3) nonprofit organization.

Emergency Support Teams, 42 U.S.C. Chapter 68, Subchapter III, § 5144. The President shall form emergency support teams of Federal personnel to be deployed in an area affected by a major disaster or emergency. The teams shall assist the Federal Coordinating Officer in carrying out his or her responsibilities pursuant to this chapter. The President may request the head of any Federal agency to detail to temporary duty with the emergency support teams personnel believed to be necessary or useful for carrying out the functions of the teams. The detail can be on either a reimbursable or non-reimbursable basis, as determined necessary by the President, and each such detail is to be without loss of seniority, pay, or other employee status.

www.ingramcontent.com/pod-product-compliance
Lightning Source LLC
Chambersburg PA
CBHW080259290526
45790CB00005B/1868